THE WORLD HAS
A BIG BACKYARD

THE WORLD HAS A BIG BACKYARD

by Mike Day

The World Has a Big Backyard © copyright 2023 by Mike Day. All rights reserved. No part of this book may be reproduced in any form whatsoever, by photography or xerography or by any other means, by broadcast or transmission, by translation into any kind of language, nor by recording electronically or otherwise, without permission in writing from the author, except by a reviewer, who may quote brief passages in critical articles or reviews.

ISBN 13: 978-1-63489-625-2

Library of Congress Catalog Number has been applied for.
Printed in the United States of America
First Printing: 2023
27 26 25 24 23   5 4 3 2 1

Cover design by Victoria Petelin
Cover photo of the Namib Desert by Mal Wolfe
IMAX® is a registered trademark of IMAX Corporation
Interior design by Vivian Steckline

Wise Ink Creative Publishing
807 Broadway St. NE, Suite 46
Minneapolis, MN 55413
wiseink.com

To order, visit itascabooks.com or call 1-800-901-3480. Reseller discounts available.

TABLE OF CONTENTS

PART ONE: THE BIG PICTURE

    1. Welcome the Adventure —————————— 3

    2. Respect the Place: Namibia & Botswana ————— 7

    3. Respect the People: Alaska ————————— 15

    4. Respect Yourself: Copenhagen ———————— 21

PART TWO: THE ADVENTURE TRAVELER'S MINDSET

    5. Embrace Uncertainty: Singapore ——————— 29

    6. Comfort Is Not Always King: Costa Rica ————— 33

    7. Take Risks: Kyushu ————————————— 41

    8. Embrace Familiarity: Hong Kong ——————— 49

    9. Adopt a Road Warrior: Greenland ——————— 55

    10. Practice Mindfulness: Tanzania ——————— 65

PART THREE: WHAT TO SEEK

    11. Seek Culture: Valencia ——————————— 81

    12. Seek Authenticity: Stockholm & Amsterdam ——— 85

    13. Seek the Locals' Favorites: Tokyo ——————— 91

    14. Don't Fear a Wrong Turn: Montgomery & Iceland — 99

PART FOUR: BRINGING IT ALL BACK HOME

15. Go Navy: Pensacola —————————————— 111
16. The Great American Eclipse: Nebraska ———————— 119
17. Storm Chasing: Tornado Alley ————————————— 131
18. Conservation Country: Wisconsin ———————————— 137
19. The Pleasantest Sensation in the World: Minnesota — 149

HUMANS NEED TO GO BEYOND THE MOUNTAINS AND VALLEYS AND THROUGH THE SCENERY THAT FILLS THEIR VIEW. OTHERWISE WE WILL NEVER FIND ANYTHING, EVEN THOUGH WE CAN SEE.

ABDUQADIR JALALIDIN
UYGHUR PROFESSOR AND POET

TRUST THAT LIFE IS A JOURNEY AND ONE THING WILL LEAD TO THE NEXT AND YOU ARE EXACTLY WHERE YOU NEED TO BE.

LP GIOBBI
PIANIST, PRODUCER, AND WORLD-TOURING DJ

VISITOR'S ENTRY PERMIT
Immigration Control Act, 1993
(Sections 9 and 29/Regulation 2)

Authorised in terms of Act 7 of 1993 for the purpose of visit/tourism/business for a period not exceeding 90 calendar days as from the date of entry. Employment in any form is prohibited.

IMMIGRATION OFFICER
VP-16

Republic of Namibia — Immigration Control — ENTRY STAMP — 22 MAR 1995 — EROS AIRPORT

IMMIGRATION SERVICE — DEPARTED 4 DEC 1985 (2100) HONG KONG

DIRECCION GEN. DE MIGR. — SALIDA — VALENCIA — 14.3.91

Misbruik / Permitted to re... until — 30 DEC 1991

For visit / Vir besoek — Purpose of visit may not be changed / Doel van besoek mag nie verander word nie

25. MAR. 1988 — COSTA RICA

01

THE BIG PICTURE

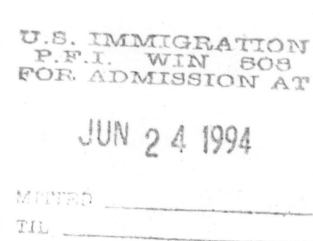

Chapter 1

WELCOME THE ADVENTURE

ANTHONY BOURDAIN, BELOVED AMERICAN chef, author, and world traveler, said it best, "If I'm an advocate for anything, it is to move. As far as you can, as much as you can. Travel isn't always pretty. It isn't always comfortable. But that's OK. The journey changes you; it should change you. Travel is about the gorgeous feeling of teetering in the unknown."

As children we have an innate curiosity about the world—fantasies of adventure. So why, when we become adults, do we prefer the easy trip to more adventurous travel? Why go to an amusement park when we can go see an active volcano?

Why? Because as we grow into adulthood, we adopt more survival instincts. Contemplating adventure travel in faraway places magnifies those instincts. We become uneasy with the idea of conversing with strangers whose language we do not speak, finding our way around in a place we have never been, making mistakes, getting lost, and the risk of being a long way from home if something happens.

Despite the risks, I believe the best gift you can give yourself, and to others, is travel. Not the typical trip. Not comfortable travel. But a trip that instills a feeling of teetering in the unknown. Adventure travel can have an enormous impact on a young person. For example, how did Dani Lacy, a girl growing up in Ohio—more than five hundred miles from an ocean—become a marine biologist?

I met Dani Lacy in Florida when she led a nature walk along the Gulf of Mexico. She told me that when she was thirteen years old, she went on a family vacation from her home in Ohio to the Bahamas. She took a scuba diving lesson along with her dad and never looked back. She went on to major in biology at Wittenberg University in Springfield, Ohio. Then she earned a master's degree specializing in tropical marine ecosystem management and marine conservation.

Another example is Gina Moseley, who I worked with on a film project. As a young teenager growing up in England, she went on a family camping trip. Gina's mother, the adventurous one in the family, signed them up for a day in Goatchurch Cavern in the limestone hills south of Bristol, an accessible cavern that provides a cave experience where one can get muddy but doesn't need special equipment. Gina remembered how much fun she had doing a "superman squeeze" (with one arm above her head and one below) to get through a narrow passageway.

Today, Dr. Gina Moseley, a professor at the University of Innsbruck and a Rolex Award Laureate, is a paleoclimatologist. She leads teams into caves around the world to collect geologic specimens, which provide a record that maps the climate history of the planet over the last half million years.

Dr. Margot Sunderland, the director of education and training at the Centre for Child Mental Health in London, has said, "An enriched environment offers new experiences that are strong in combined social, physical, cognitive and sensory interaction. If you are choosing between buying your child a tablet or taking them on a family holiday, consider the profound effects on bonding and brain development—there is no competition." The amount of enrichment from the purchase of a new thing wanes over time, whereas the experiences that travel provides—create memories that can last a lifetime.

I was privileged to enjoy a life of world travel making documentary films in the world's largest film format—the IMAX® format. Filmmaker Dennis Earl Moore told *InPark* magazine, "It was fantastic, sitting there in an IMAX theater, surrounded by imagery—it was a complete, visual experience that was unprecedented. It brought documentary filmmaking to bigger audiences—it was about place, the idea of going someplace and being immersed in an environment."

As the executive producer of more than a dozen documentary films, I had the opportunity to bring stories to a giant screen that captured experiences few people ever have, and to bring audiences to places they would otherwise never see. The best part of the job was traveling to so many distant places. Through those experiences, I learned that travel helps us develop skills to address the uncertainty, unpredictability, uncontrollability, and anxiety that come not just in traveling, but in everyday life. You don't travel only to get better at traveling; you travel to better face a world where you can't control all the variables.

There is no better enrichment experience than travel that pushes us outside of our comfort zones to witness the unfamiliar, explore the unknown, question our assumptions, and confront our anxieties. By sticking with the familiar we might feel bigger, but we are left smaller because we have limited our opportunities to grow. Exposure to more of the world increases our humanity. As Bourdain said, "The journey changes you; it should change you."

The question, "Why go to an amusement park when we can go see an active volcano?" is symbolic of the idea of going to any number of worldwide places for authentic experiences that will ignite the senses, spark wonder, stretch your understanding of self, and make you muse.

THE BIG PICTURE

The definition of muse is "to think deeply." When you put an "a" in front of a word it negates its meaning. Thus, amusement means "not to think deeply."

Don't travel to amuse. Travel to muse.

The world has a big backyard.

Chapter 2

RESPECT THE PLACE

NAMIBIA & BOTSWANA

I LED A FILM team on a scouting trip through southern Africa for the making of a film entitled *The Greatest Places*. We were looking to film magnificent manifestations of the physical geography of our planet. We anticipated filming in serene environments, but came to discover, repeatedly, that it is a challenging and precarious world. And the critical lesson for working in that world was to have respect for it.

One target for this project was to film one of the most unique and extraordinary rivers on earth—the Okavango. Most rivers run into another body of water: a lake, an ocean, another river. However, unlike the Nile River, which drains into the Mediterranean Sea, or the Mississippi River, which flows into the Gulf of Mexico, the Okavango does not drain into another body of water—it fans out over a 150-square-mile area of the Kalahari Desert in Botswana.

My time in the Okavango was mesmerizing. Sunlight glistened off the rivulets and marshes of a vast riverway that ran to nowhere. There were birds and beasts I had only seen in books, and many I couldn't recognize at all. Every day in the delta felt like I was falling into the pages of *National Geographic*.

My trip to the Okavango was my first "safari," an expedition to view the natural wonders of Africa. There is little human presence in the Okavango, but a great deal of wildlife. Our guide was anxious for us to see Africa's most iconic animals, known as the Big Five: the elephant, the rhino, the leopard, the cape buffalo, and the lion. The Big Five are a holdover from an age when a safari meant hunting wild animals with guns instead of cameras. These five trophy species do not include some of the most magnificent animals of Africa's wild kingdom, such as hippos, giraffes, and wild dogs, which we would encounter on this trip. While reading about a member of a canoe trip who was taken out by a hippo on the Zambezi River where I had canoed the week before, I learned that hippos kill more humans than any of the Big Five.

The film's director, producer, and me, the executive producer of the project, were escorted around the inland Okavango River delta by a guide in a well-worn safari vehicle. It was closed-sided with three rows of seating, no roof, and roll bars. Our guide and director sat in the front, the producer sat in the middle row, and I stood in the back hanging on to the roll bar. As we passed a line of trees to our left, I spotted a pair of elephants moving in the same direction as we were. Our guide said there was a clearing ahead where we could stop and wait for the elephants to arrive. What we found when we stopped wasn't a pair of elephants, but nearly a hundred of them.

Elephants travel in herds led by a matriarch, usually the oldest female. A herd is made up of daughters, sisters, and their offspring. Male elephants stay with the herd through adolescence and then move away. Herds consist of dozens of elephants, and during a day, sometimes herds conjoin.

I was struck by how quiet this elephant herd was as they passed. I guess I had expected that, given their size, elephants' feet would make a loud stomping sound as they walked. What I found was quite the opposite. The soft padding on the underside of their feet allowed them to move almost silently. Given they only sleep a few hours each night, elephant herds are on the move for long days, and their trunks almost always are in motion. Standing in the back of a vehicle as scores of elephants quietly walked around me, trunks swaying, I felt as if I were on stage during a ballet with the world's largest land mammal.

Later that day as we drove back to camp, we approached a pack of wild dogs lying about. The primary commandment of travel was paramount at this moment; respect the world around you. In this case, that meant respect the wildlife. Our guide cautioned us to keep our hands and arms in the truck. As passive as they appeared, these were not the kind of dogs you pet. We watched as one rose and started "twittering." More joined in, touching their noses together and making high pitched sounds before they dashed off as a pack. Our guide explained that this was their behavior when rallying for a hunt.

Late that afternoon, we stopped at a watering hole and watched as another herd of elephants made its way toward us. They ambled without interruption on the other side of the Okavango lagoon. Though we were hot, dry, and dusty from a day of safari, our guide warned us not to get any ideas about going for a dip. As the sun set, we discovered the wisdom of his advice when a peaceful-looking landscape revealed itself to be otherwise. A pair of eyes popped out of the water. That pair was followed by another, and another, and a dozen more—crocodiles.

African freshwater crocodiles are aggressive, with a powerful bite, sharp conical teeth, and a strong grip that allows them to hold down their victims underwater to drown. They are ambush predators who will wait hours—even days—for the moment to attack.

Our guide told us the story of one of the most horrific crocodile attacks ever reported, which happened in the Democratic Republic of the Congo to two world-class kayakers, Chris Korbulic and Ben Stookesberry. The pair met in Oregon at the screening of a kayaking film and developed a friendship that took them to rivers in Bhutan, Argentina, Canada, Pakistan, and elsewhere around the world. In 2010, they headed off for a trip on the Congo's Lukuga River. Their expedition was led by Hendrik Coetzee, a thirty-five-year-old South African living in Uganda who was regarded as the premier kayaker in Africa. He was a legend. Celliers Kruger, owner of a South African kayaking company, said about Coetzee, "He was very calculated and set the bar high for exploration in Africa."

All three kayakers were experts at running whitewater rapids. The Americans planned to film the trip on the Lukuga, a river whose navigation had never been documented. After weeks of preparation, the three kayakers launched their expedition.

The Lukuga River includes one forty-mile stretch of rapids, which the group navigated in their first days on the river. Having navigated the last expected rapids, they started out early the next morning. They spotted a few small crocodiles along the way. As experienced kayakers, they cautiously paddled their three kayaks in a tight formation so they would look like one big creature to any potential predator. Hendrik Coetzee led the way when disaster struck. Chris Korbulic only saw the flash of the giant jaws of a crocodile as it leapt from the water and grabbed Coetzee. The crocodile pulled him out of sight, never to be seen again.

The American kayakers raced ahead a mile to a village on the shore. Minutes later, Coetzee's empty boat floated by. Stookesberry later spoke of the tragedy, saying, "Before we could even react, the kayak was almost submerged. When it came back up, it rocked slightly to reveal an empty cockpit. The attack was like lightning striking. I didn't understand how something that big could have come out of that river without us having any inkling."

RESPECT THE PLACE

THE MORNING FOLLOWING MY first crocodile sighting, I strolled with our guide from our campsite in Botswana to a nearby lagoon to enjoy our morning coffee and the serenity of a cool Okavango morning. On the other side of the pond we saw a pack of wild dogs chasing, but not catching, a herd of impalas. They all ran off beyond our view, but one of the impalas had chosen to run into the water as its defense against the dogs. It stood in water up to its chest, frozen with fear. As the expert of our group, our guide said something that I understood from our experience the evening before. He muttered, "That critter is in deep shit."

We waited. Before long, a pair of eyes popped up from the water and began moving toward the hind end of the impala. The crocodile picked up speed as its jaws widened to bite deep into the animal's haunch. Then it swam off, leaving its quarry bleeding profusely.

Another set of eyes appeared, following a similar path and moving at a greater speed than the first. We stood silent, holding our coffee cups, and bearing witness to a pending evisceration. This croc moved with remarkable speed as it leapt from the water, clamped its jaws around the impala's neck, and did a mid-air twist to snap the neck of the already bloodied prey.

Welcome to breakfast in the Okavango.

OUR FILM SCOUTING TRIP moved from the Okavango River delta in Botswana to the country to the west, Namibia. It is one of three places on earth that have the right alignment to create a hyper-arid desert right next to an ocean: Mexico's Baja Peninsula, Chile's Atacama, and the Namib Desert in Namibia.

While the Namib Desert is dry with rare rainfall, its west coast on the Atlantic Ocean has a cold-water current that makes conditions ripe for dense fog. Published photos of decaying

THE BIG PICTURE

shipwrecks, and the supposed remains of shipwreck-stranded sailors who met their demise trying to survive in the desert, inspired the area's name: Skeleton Coast.

The Namib has the tallest sand dunes on earth, carved by wind from the coast. Millions of years old, the sand has a distinctive red color from iron oxide. People often look at pictures of this part of the world and mistake it for the surface of Mars.

At the Namib-Naukluft National Park you can visit, and climb, these extraordinary sand dunes. The park is open from sunrise to sunset. The most spectacular dunes are deep inside the park, including one of the most visited and photographed—Dune 45, so named as it is forty-five kilometers from the park entrance.

GOING ON SAFARI TO multiple locations in Africa means you will be passed from guide to guide, from your primary contracted outfitter to a series of subcontractors. For our four-wheel driving trip through Namibia, we had a commanding German guide with a thick accent, who carried a Luger.

From 1884, Namibia was a German colony. That history is still apparent in its architecture, restaurants, street names, and annual Oktoberfest. Less visible is the memory of the German genocide of the Herero and Nama people in the first decade of the twentieth century. Almost half of the Nama and 80 percent of the Herero were killed. In 1990 the country won independence and became the Republic of Namibia.

We told our guide we wanted to scout deep within the park at first light in consideration of filming at that time. So, at the end of our first day, we parked our vehicle within the park and hiked back to our camp. Our guide told us we could retrieve our vehicle early next morning. This meant we would be in the park when we were not supposed to be there. Our guide said we should stop at the park headquarters after scouting and pay our daily admission fee, but warned us that we would get in trouble for trespassing in the park before it opened.

When we went to the park headquarters at the end of the day, two employees, one white, one Black, sat at side-by-side desks. It appeared to manifest a transition underway in Namibia. The white employee was a vestige of apartheid, which restricted the majority-Black population from social and economic opportunity. The other employee manifested the country's progression past its history of extreme racial segregation. The Black park employee and our German guide did all the talking and were somewhat antagonistic toward each other.

I interrupted: "You guys need to buy a bus and charge people a high price to drive them into the park to climb Dune 45 and watch the sunrise." Before I could suggest they set up a coffee cart on the bus and upsell their customers, our German guide jumped up and pulled me to the back of the room. "Shut up," he warned me, "unless you want to get us arrested."

That day I learned an invaluable travel and life lesson: be respectful of the places you visit. Being in the park headquarters in the Namib Desert, I was at the mercy of the park employee's good graces, hopeful he would overlook my trespasses. It was time to respect the place and its people, to listen, and to learn, not pitch a new park business plan.

Chapter 3

RESPECT THE PEOPLE

Alaska

THE PEOPLE OF ALASKA, known for their independence, have a certain mystique. Perhaps due to a perception that they live in isolation in frontier settings, enduring the hardship of long, cold winters.

Russia sold Alaska to the United States in 1867. In 1959, it became the forty-ninth state. Alaska has an area that is more than the total of the next three largest states combined: Texas, California, and Montana. However, the population of those three states is one hundred times that of Alaska, and half of Alaskans live in the Anchorage area. That leaves more than 660,000 square miles for the rest of Alaskans to live on.

Commercial oil exploration began in Alaska in the 1960s. In 1968, the discovery at Prudhoe Bay led to the construction of the Trans-Alaska Pipeline. The pipeline could not be built, as written in the newsletter *Indian Affairs*, without addressing the "traditional use and occupancy" of land by native populations. In 1971, Congress passed the Alaska Native Claims Settlement Act. It paid $962,500,000 for native claims to Alaska's land. The oil boom allowed the state to repeal its income tax, and there is no statewide sales tax.

One spring my spouse and I made our first trip to Alaska. We got good advice to not try and see and do too much in the ten days we had for our trip. We flew from Minneapolis to

Anchorage and rented a four-wheel-drive Chevy Suburban. We took out the third row of seats in case we needed to sleep in the vehicle. Most visitors drive north from Anchorage to see Denali, the highest mountain peak in North America. We were advised to avoid that drive up the "tourist highway" as we might not see much of the mountain because of weather. So, we headed south out of Anchorage to explore and camp in the Kenai Peninsula.

The key item for driving Alaska is *The Milepost* travel guide, the bible of Alaska travel since 1949. Since much of Alaska is reached by one road, including from Anchorage onto the Kenai Peninsula, you don't look for addresses. Everything is noted by its milepost—mileage markers along the way. *The Milepost* is like the Yellow Pages of everything in Alaska, noting at what mile you will find it. Even in the digital age, a hard copy is a highly recommended item.

Kris Valencia, the longtime editor of *The Milepost*, regarded the Seward Highway from Anchorage onto the Kenai Peninsula as the most scenic drive in Alaska. The 125-mile stretch of road was built in 1951. It runs through the Chugach National Forest, the Kenai Mountains, and along the Turnagain Arm. The longtime *Milepost* editor's advice for first-time visitors to the state? "Take it slow. When you take it slow, it is an epiphany."

The Cook Inlet separates the Kenai Peninsula from the mainland. A branch of the inlet at the north end is the Turnagain Arm. It has the largest tides in the United States, which rise up to forty feet. In 1778, British Captain James Cook brought two ships into the inlet looking for a route back to Europe, a "Northwest Passage." He sailed into the waterway, but his crew exploring in small boats discovered it was not open to the east. He was forced to turn around, or "turn again," a name that stuck with the inlet.

The Great Alaska Earthquake happened on Good Friday in 1964. The land around the Turnagain Arm sank from the earthquake, leaving behind an expanse of mudflats. There is no hiking here. When the tide comes in the mud is like quicksand.

The Seward Highway runs along the north side of the Turnagain Arm. Unfortunately, one of the highway's highlights, the Bird House Bar in Bird Creek, burned down in 1996. The bar was easy to spot because it had a big blue papier-mâché bird sticking out of the peak of the uninsulated log cabin. The interior of the bar was covered with things people had stapled to the walls and ceiling—money, draft cards, photos, divorce papers, even underwear. Opened in 1963, the bar was small, intimate, and unique. It began tilting the year after it opened as the ground sank during the Great Alaska Earthquake. When you sat at the Bird House Bar, you sat at an angle.

When we drove onto the Peninsula in May, there were fifty-foot-high snowbanks on either side of the highway, cut out by snow removal crews. During winter along the Seward Highway, snow and ice removal can be limited, as are gasoline and cell phone coverage. When we drove it in early May, there was virtually no traffic; the start of the salmon fishing and tourist season was still a couple of weeks away. The Kenai culture is distinct. A home is not highlighted by a yard of grass, but rather a yard of gravel with a collection of heavy metal objects: old buses, cement mixers, satellite dishes. Wealth is having a freezer full of hunted or trapped wild game.

Respecting people as you travel, and making you more comfortable in a distant place, supports dressing as the locals do. On the peninsula no one is alarmed if you wear a Bowie knife and bear bells. Think of the big jingle bells that Santa would hang from the reindeer that pulled his sleigh. On the Peninsula, you wear a string of those off your belt to scare the bears off before they see you.

Learning about the people and lifestyle that you will encounter in traveling demonstrates further respect. A seasoned

Alaska traveler told us we might encounter "survivor syndrome" among the locals. Alaskans living on the Kenai Peninsula spend long winter months isolated from those coming from elsewhere. Every time we encountered a Peninsula resident, their first question was "Where ya' from?" From our experienced Alaska traveler, we learned Alaskans weren't interested in whether we were from outside of Alaska, so we always responded with "Down from Anchorage." Their reply was always the same. Their mouths and eyes would widen and they'd say, "Oh, the road is open!" We were the first people they had seen from off the Peninsula since the winter locked them down. Their primary interest was in learning from us that the roadway could now be traveled to Anchorage. We respected their months of isolation by providing them the one key piece of information they wanted and nothing more.

The Seward Highway takes you to Seward, a fishing town along the south shore of the Peninsula on the Gulf of Alaska's Resurrection Bay. This is a part of the world where you want to get off the road and on the water—or in the air. We went to a "Flight See" office one morning to see this spectacular part of the world from above. As we were ahead of the season, the office said they weren't booking tours yet. They suggested coming back that afternoon as they had a training session for a new pilot and we could buy a ride. Even though the veteran pilot was unimpressed with the new pilot, which made our ride feel like sitting in the back seat listening to a couple argue in the front, it was a phenomenal flight experience with extraordinary views.

The Kenai Fjords National Park covers more than 600,000 acres in this part of the Peninsula, with three dozen glaciers coming down from the Harding Ice Field. You can drive up to one of the glaciers, take a strenuous hike on the Harding Ice Field Trail, or even camp along it. Instead, we flew over it on our flight see—or *part* of it. When we were there, the ice field was seven hundred square miles.

Our driving trip took us nearly two hundred miles from Seward to the western end of the Peninsula and the town of Homer. I planned a camping night there on the public beach at the end of the Homer Spit. The Spit is a five-mile-long piece of land jutting into the Kachemak Bay. As we drove by the Salty Dawg Saloon, two members of a fishing crew crashed out of the door throwing fists at each other. We didn't stay to see who won the fight. Instead, we crossed the Salty Dawg off our list of things to do on the Homer Spit.

The campsite was a gravel beach. Thousands of seabirds squawked all night, hoping to get the remnants from the popular halibut fishing tours or the commercial canning company across the road. My spouse still maintains the hum from the canning factory, the noisy birds, and tent camping on a gravel bed in the Land of the Midnight Sun were grounds for divorce.

The Milepost informed me of a laundromat up the road from Homer where, in addition to washing your clothes, you could also take a hot shower for only $1. It made for a good date, shoring up our marriage after the night on the Spit. As I stood under the stream of water I reveled in the simple pleasure of a shower, far from a spa-like setting. I thought of how Alaskans valued a full freezer and an open road. How the fundamentals of humanity, and our respect for them, are the true values that make us rich. In clean clothes with washed hair and clean bodies, we put on our bear bells and Bowie knives and headed back up the road.

As we made our way back to Anchorage, I wondered what they would say back home if I wore my Bowie knife and bear bells and jingle-jangled into a 7-Eleven gas station convenience store. I wondered if they would simply think, "Oh, the road is open."

Chapter 4

RESPECT YOURSELF

COPENHAGEN

I ARRIVED IN DENMARK on a beautiful spring afternoon in May. I purposely arrived one day early before beginning my business.

Stephanie Korpal, a mental health therapist, was quoted on her website as saying, "I like to recommend people spend quiet time transitioning to being in a new space once they arrive at their destination. It can be critical to slow down and let our emotional selves catch up to our physical selves." I have found this valuable travel self-care advice, for both leisure and business sojourns. Give yourself some time and space to adjust to a new setting before asking more of yourself and others.

When I came to Copenhagen, the time we lived by printed guidebooks and maps was past. Now all that information is on our smartphones. Walking tours of the world's great cities are there. We don't have to struggle with figuring out if we're heading in the right direction. That pulsing blue dot on our phone map moves with us. When it indicates we're going in the wrong direction, we simply turn around, or better yet, we surrender to going in the unintended direction to see what lies ahead.

More people travel by bike than by car in Copenhagen. Judging by the number of bicyclists, I quickly discerned what is an honest fear for a traveler new to Copenhagen: stepping in front of a moving bike. In my first minutes on the streets of Copenhagen, I stepped off a curb while paying close attention to my phone—too close. I was almost hit by a bicyclist. I leapt back on the curb, reminded myself to slow down, and paused to assess my surroundings.

They say a great way to see Copenhagen is to rent a bike, which comes with the advice to also rent a helmet. I chose to go slower. To let my emotional self catch up with my physical self. As I was in the first hours of my first visit to this country, I stayed off the bikeways and instead took a walk.

I found my way to Nyhavn, the harbor of Copenhagen. Along the canal are the oft photographed multicolored seventeenth- and eighteenth-century townhomes. Hans Christian Andersen lived in one when he wrote *The Princess and the Pea*. The neighborhood, with its wooden ships and cafes and restaurants, is rated near the top of any list of things to do in Copenhagen. I found it to be an ideal place to experience at a slower pace, and boarded a canalboat for an hour-long tour that provided a good introduction to the city in both Danish and English.

On my walkabout, I stumbled into the infamous Freetown Christiania section of the city. Established in the early 1970s, Christiania has been known as the cannabis trade zone; a self-governing, self-sustaining enclave; an expression of a free society; a rebellion against bureaucracy; a car-free communal neighborhood, and much more. They fly their own flag. Tourism and gentrification have changed the neighborhood that was known as a free lifestyle zone. Jorgen Jensen, who came to live in Christiania when he was seventeen and stayed more than forty-five years, said, "It's simply too expensive to be a Christiania hippie these days."

Sitting for a quiet, light meal is one more way to both slow down and begin immersion into a new place, a new culture. As Copenhagen sits on a strait of water connecting the North

RESPECT YOURSELF

Sea with the Baltic Sea, it is resplendent with seafood. A standard lunch meal is an open-faced sandwich on dark Danish rye bread, topped with cold salmon, roast beef with fried onions, chicken salad with bacon, or pickled herring. For lunch I opted for a topping of hard-boiled egg with shrimp.

Copenhagen's penchant for bikes is more than for convenience. It is one element in their dedication to a sustainable lifestyle. In addition to a continued commitment to bicycle travel, Copenhagen has one of the world's best public transport networks of buses, trains, and metro rapid transit. It reduced its carbon emissions by more than 25 percent in a ten-year period beginning in 2005. Ninety percent of building waste is recycled or reused. The city buys more organic food than any other capital city, and almost all the food served in municipal institutions is organic. Already, most of Denmark's use of electricity comes from wind or solar sources. Copenhagen has the most aggressive carbon neutrality goal of any city on Earth.

IN THE FIRST DECADE of the twenty-first century, the transition from film-based technology to digital technology swept around the world. IMAX had thrived for forty years as the superior capture and projection technology for film. The challenge was to maintain that quality during the evolution of technology. A new generation of Canadian engineers and innovators channeled the same spirit and dedication that created the IMAX film format to create a giant screen digital projection system—IMAX with laser illumination.

I was in Copenhagen to attend a technology demonstration set up by IMAX engineers in cooperation with the Tycho Brahe Planetarium. Also among the attendees was a colleague who operated a successful IMAX Dome Theater in The Hague, and the CEO of the Tycho Brahe. We viewed a prototype for what would become the IMAX laser-illuminated digital dome projection system, the best giant screen experience in the world.

Taking a day for myself prior to my business in Copenhagen provided me an opportunity to start to see and know the place and develop an appreciation for it. It left me refreshed for a full day of business in meetings with engineers and museum professionals, including multi-hours of technical conversation that continued through dinner.

That evening, we were guests of the Tycho Brahe CEO for dinner. He took us to Tivoli Gardens, what I heard was an amusement park. Since Copenhagen has more than two thousand restaurants, I was surprised we would have dinner at an amusement park. I discovered that calling Tivoli Gardens an amusement park is a misnomer. It has rides, unique in their design, including a wooden roller coaster from 1914. But Tivoli, which opened in the 1840s, is much more than that. It is a festival of events and performances, parades, restaurants, beer halls, music, games, and gardens. I was glad we came for dinner and then a walkthrough. A large crowd had come for a live concert. I didn't speak the language so I couldn't sing along in Dutch, but I did share a great sense of community, and the lights of the Tivoli at night were stunning.

VISITOR'S ENTRY PERMIT

Immigration Control Act, 1993
(Sections 9 and 29/Regulation 2)

Authorised in terms of Act 7 of 1993 for the purpose of visit/tourism/business for a period not exceeding 90 calendar days as from the date of entry. Employment in any form is prohibited.

IMMIGRATION OFFICER

VT-16

Republic of Namibia — Immigration Control
ENTRY STAMP
2 2 MAR 1995
EOS AIRPORT

IMMIGRATION SERVICE
4 DEC 1985
DEPARTED (2100)
HONG KONG

DIRECCIÓN GRAL. DE MIGRACIÓN
FRONTERA
14.3.04
SALIDA

Visit not permitted to re... until 3 0 DEC 1991

FOR VISIT / VIR BESOEK
PURPOSE OF VISIT MAY NOT BE CHANGED/DOEL VAN BESOEK MAG NIE VERANDER WORD NIE

25 MAR 1988
COSTA RICA

02

THE ADVENTURE TRAVELER'S MINDSET

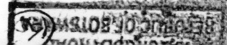

Chapter 5

EMBRACE UNCERTAINTY

SINGAPORE

UPON MY FIRST-EVER ARRIVAL in Singapore I felt like I was looking at a painting from antiquity being lacquered over with a modernistic brush. It appeared to be a place minimizing its past while constructing a modern Shangri-la. I was overwhelmed and disoriented with my immersion into a place that felt so different, so ambiguous, a place so hyper-modern, clean, orderly, and disciplined.

Singapore may be the cleanest city-state on the planet, even with one of the greatest population densities on Earth. A look back at not-so-distant history explains a few of the reasons. In 1992, the distribution of chewing gum was banned. In 1994, a teenager at the Singapore American School was arrested for vandalism and sentenced to caning, a legacy of British colonial rule. The American received four strokes of a thick palm cane across his bare back. Visitors to Singapore are advised to not jaywalk, chew gum, feed pigeons, or spit in public—offenses that can carry a hefty fine.

In 1819, Sir Stamford Raffles established Singapore as a British Empire trading post. It was occupied by the Japanese during World War II but returned to British control after the war. In 1959, it became a self-governing independent country.

In 1965, Lee Kuan Yew, a young lawyer, became the Republic of Singapore's first prime minister. He directed Singapore for the next forty years. His economic and social planning was for the long term. He made English the "common language" to allow for world trade, but mandated bilingualism in schools to preserve the language and ethnicity of Singapore—keeping one foot in the past while the other races forward.

Without any natural resources of its own, Singapore became a major financial and shipping center with outstanding education and healthcare facilities. It has the world's highest percentage of millionaires. More than 90 percent of Singaporeans are homeowners, and they have one of the world's longest life expectancies and lowest infant mortality rates.

I had to go to Singapore, where a US colleague of mine was working on a project that had taken him in and out of the country. A few weeks before my own trip, I called him to get travel tips and gain some clarity about the culture of the place. This was in the days before smartphones, text messages, and email. I couldn't reach my contact, so I left him a voicemail message asking him to call me back. Before I boarded my flight, I received a message from him. He was in Singapore and I was to call him upon my arrival.

My uncertainty with the country was manifested upon my first steps into Singapore's Changi Airport, which is part airport, part luxury mall, and part rainforest. Travel writer Nomadic Matt called it "airport heaven." In one terminal, a giant kinetic sculpture hypnotizes viewers. In another terminal, a thousand droplets, each coated with polished copper, form different flying themed shapes. The installation represents the rain that falls in this tropical country, which lies one degree north of the equator. The airport has a donut-shaped glass and steel dome with 280 shops circling the perimeter. In the middle of this stands the tallest indoor waterfall in the world. At night, it acts as a canvas for a light show.

After arriving at my hotel, my colleague came by to take me around. We went to the Raffles Hotel, which opened in 1887. It remains a display of historic Singapore with its Renaissance revival architecture, high ceilings, extensive verandas, a timber staircase, teakwood floors, and handmade carpets. In 1902, a tiger strolled into the hotel's bar and fell asleep under a billiard table.

We slunk into bamboo chairs to drink the national cocktail—a Singapore Sling. It was created around 1915 by Ngiam Tong Boon, a bartender at the Raffles Hotel. No two recipes read alike, but the foundation is two measures of gin and one of cherry brandy, with an assortment of fruit juices shaken with ice to create a foamy top. The bartender who served us told us he was related to Ngiam Tong Boon. I believe every bartender at the Raffles Hotel is trained to say they are related to Ngiam Tong Boon.

To my surprise, a young local woman joined us. Though she was apparently a cohort of my colleague, I was never told how they had met or what she did for a living, but she became our guide for the afternoon—an afternoon that taught me that when you go with the flow and embrace uncertainty, good things might happen.

As we walked down a street full of newer retail shops, my colleague opened the door into a shop empty except for broken glass and shelving, the remnants of an abandoned retail operation. Without hesitation, he headed to the back of the shop and opened a door to a back room. There, a local set up peg boards where he sold imitation watches. For $12, I bought a beautiful Rolex knockoff that worked well for the many years I wore it. A coworker once told me she thought my watch was cool. I admitted to her that it wasn't a real Rolex and I told her how I acquired it. She thought it was even cooler that I had to go to Singapore to get it.

When we arrived in Chinatown, we sat in a wet market along a stall with fresh feathered and headless chickens hanging from a rack. The term "wet market" originated in Singapore in the 1970s. The wet refers to the floors of the market, which are wet from melting ice and the washing of poultry and meat in food stalls. The seafood wet market in Wuhan, China, is believed to have been the source of the worldwide COVID-19 pandemic. The SARS outbreak was also linked to such a market.

This part of Singapore felt like it was intentionally segregated from "modern" Singapore to maintain a connection to the city's cultural past. Being there felt like being in a Somerset Maugham novel. Maugham was famous for novels published in the 1920s and 30s that portrayed the late days of European colonialism in Southeast Asia. He came to Singapore in 1921 and lived at the Raffles Hotel.

Singapore's wet market provided me a valuable lesson to help manage the uneasiness of distant travel and sudden immersion into a different place. The lesson is: challenge your need for clarity by learning to tolerate, even embrace, the inevitable uncertainty of life. Recognize there will be moments where it is best to surrender to the world's unpredictability.

We drank several bottles of Tiger Beer. We smoked cigarettes. I even saw someone spit on the ground. Between the jet lag, the alcohol, our young companion, and my new Rolex watch, I became comfortable with my disorientation and surrendered to the all-consuming "gorgeous feeling of teetering in the unknown."

Chapter 6

COMFORT IS NOT ALWAYS KING

Costa Rica

I HAVE ALWAYS TOLD film students that the hardest job on a film project is that of the producer. The producer must make everything work when a film crew is on location. A film crew needs comfortable beds to sleep in. They must have access to clean bathrooms. They need to be fed. They need to stay healthy. They will be working with technical equipment, which necessitates access to people and hardware to solve any challenge. The producer is responsible for the logistics of moving people and equipment, while keeping everything working on time and on budget. They must get along with everybody, and they strive to help everybody get along with everyone else.

I have also told students I preferred the responsibility I had as executive producer, especially when scouting film locations. Scouting takes us around the world to decide where and what the crew will ultimately record. Scouting means visiting more locations than end up in a finished film.

During scouting, a producer takes copious notes about how logistics will be managed, including the housing and feeding of a film crew for multiple weeks, as well as how much everything will cost in terms of time and money. An executive producer looks around a lot. The big decision the executive producer must ultimately face is if the project is viable. Can it be pulled off, will audiences be interested, and, most importantly, can it be financed and then provide a return on the investment.

DURING A SCOUTING TRIP for an IMAX film on tropical rainforests, my selected director and producer and I hired an ornithologist and her spouse, a biologist, to take us through Costa Rica, an anticipated primary location for the film. Costa Rica is Spanish for "rich coast." It has two: the Pacific Ocean is on the west coast, and the Caribbean Sea is on the east.

If you are at a high northern latitude such as the Canadian province of Manitoba, you will find two dozen native species of trees. As you travel south, that number increases. By the time you reach Costa Rica in Central America, you will find almost two thousand species of trees. This pattern holds true across nonmigratory life forms on Earth. In Manitoba you can identify thirty-seven species of butterflies. In Costa Rica there are more than 1,250. Manitoba has four species of frogs. Costa Rica has more than 150. This biological diversity is why we pay so much attention to the tropics.

Twenty-five percent of Costa Rica is held in national parks, wildlife refuges, and biological and forest preserves. Our first destination to scout was Parque Nacional Corcovado on the Osa Peninsula, which juts out into the Pacific Ocean. At the time, there were no paved roads to Corcovado and no docks to land a boat. There was a long narrow patch of forest, cut out at a right angle to the coastline, where a single engine plane could land. The runway was marked by truck tires that were painted white. There were no night landings at Corcovado. There is no airport code assigned to the place.

I remember descending over the Pacific Ocean, looking at the beautiful coastline devoid of any sign of humanity. It reminded me of Santa Monica with its sandy beaches, sunshine, and waves, except there were no houses, highways, cars, lifeguard stations, or smog, and not even one of the nearly ten million people that live in Los Angeles County. As our plane descended, the tropical forest loomed larger and larger, as did the heat and humidity.

We unpacked our gear from the plane and headed to the park headquarters. I remember pausing as our pilot turned the plane around on the runway, which was surrounded by jungle vegetation cut back with machetes to keep it useable for small aircraft. As it took off over the ocean without us, I realized that with no phones, no electronics, and no roads to anywhere, we would be out of communication with the rest of the world until an airplane would—*and could*—come back to pick us up.

Like any national park, there was a headquarters at Corcovado National Park where we had to register and pay a fee upon arrival. The park office person who met us wore a white T-shirt, shorts, tall rubber boots, and a machete on his belt. We signed the registration book. Corcovado had been a national park for ten years when we arrived; they were still using the original registration book. Its average yearly visitation in its first decade of operation was three hundred people. The average annual visitation to Yellowstone National Park in the United States is more than three million.

At the time of our film scout, most of the other visitors to Corcovado were researchers from universities from around the globe. A few university campsites were around the park headquarters. We had to bring all our provisions for our stay.

On our first afternoon, our hired scientists, both of whom had done research in Corcovado, took us on a hike. Many hours into walking in the jungle, I realized we would be hiking back after sunset. In the high northern latitudes, like the Canadian provinces and Alaska, the summer sun sets at an acute angle to the horizon and dusk can last a long time. In the tropics, like

Costa Rica at 10° north of the equator, the sun sets at an almost right angle to the horizon all year long. Dusk is short. Dark comes quickly.

Our biologist guide confirmed my suspicion when he said we would take a dinner break and watch it get dark. We pulled headlamps out of our backpacks and strapped them around our foreheads. I welcomed taking anything out of my pack because it meant I would no longer be carrying it. I was delighted to open several cans of hearts of palm I had been hauling. I was ready to eat all that I could, not because I was hungry, but to lighten the load I was carrying.

As darkness fell, the wilderness teemed with activity. Out came flying click beetles, illuminating the darkness with headlights of their own. The beetles were clumsy critters that flew until they hit a tree and fell to the ground. They have two small bioluminescent light organs at the back of their head, and unlike fireflies that flash on and off, the click beetles' headlamps remain glowing.

We watched our every step as the narrow trail was full of tarantulas. They are nocturnal—they come out at night—which is why we didn't see them on our walk into the jungle.

Bats preferred to fly the open trail, zipping by our heads. The same was true as we were sleeping on an open-air platform under the covering of a roof. We laid down on our sleeping bags with bats flying by. Instead of counting sheep, I counted bats and hoped to fall asleep quickly.

On a long hike the next day, we came upon a stream and an opening to the sky. Normally the jungle has a canopy of tropical trees that filter the sun and create patchy shadows. We took advantage of the opportunity to strip down to our underwear and cool ourselves in the knee-deep water of the stream. As we relaxed, I noticed distinct footprints in the mud on the opposite bank. I called our biologist over and pointed them out. He hunched down next to me and touched a footprint, then looked at me and whispered, "Jaguar."

With a body longer than six feet, the jaguar is the largest cat species in the Americas and a good swimmer. Its image appears widely in the culture of the Maya. Like a leopard, its pattern provides good camouflage in a shadowy jungle environment of patchy shadows. It is also a carnivore that hunts large prey like deer, agouti, giant anteaters, and cattle. I thought about this as I stood naked except for my underpants, with my feet sinking into the muddy bank of a jungle stream a long way from home. Fortunately, I didn't learn until later that jaguars are "stalk-and-ambush" hunters. They attack from cover with a quick pounce to the blind spot of their prey.

THE JAGUAR IS LISTED as a threatened species by the International Union for the Conservation of Nature, the result of a loss of habitat and cattle ranchers that know it as a threat. Alan Rabinowitz, former head of science for the Wildlife Conservation Society, made it his mission to solve this problem by establishing the Paseo del Jaguar, or Path of the Jaguar. The Paseo is an interconnected continuous conservation pathway from the United States to South America, through the jaguar's historical habitat. It allows jaguars to travel, hunt, and breed while avoiding humans and cattle.

Rabinowitz, raised in Queens, studied ecology at the University of Tennessee, where he received a master's degree and a PhD. He became one of the world's great conservationists, using his research on animals in the wild to create preserves for them. His research in Myanmar, which included the discovery of new mammal species, led to the creation of the country's largest national park, largest wildlife sanctuary, and first marine park. In Thailand, he did the first field research on tigers and leopards, leading the United Nations to declare a world heritage site there.

In his book, *Jaguar: One Man's Struggle to Establish the World's First Jaguar Preserve*, Rabinowitz describes his experience living in the tropical rainforest of Belize, where he led the establishment of the world's only jaguar preserve, the Cockscomb Basin Wildlife Sanctuary. "I realized early on in my career that the way to protect areas is to work with the sexiest, most charismatic large carnivores, which were the cats." Rabinowitz once said.

The Cockscomb Basin Wildlife Sanctuary covers 128,000 acres, including the headwaters of two major river systems and hardwood forests. It not only provides a sanctuary for the jaguar, but for the other four species of cats in Belize, as well: the jaguarundi, margay, ocelot, and puma. It is also home to tapirs, howler monkeys, and more than 290 species of birds.

IN ADDITION TO MACHETE-MAINTAINED runways, tarantulas, and jaguars, Costa Rica was also my first introduction to volcanoes. This included Arenal, a stratovolcano that stands more than a mile high and is one of the most active volcanoes in Central America. It sat quiet for generations until, in 1968, it erupted unexpectedly, as volcanoes will do. Rocks, ash, and lava destroyed three small villages. Crops were ruined, livestock perished, and more than eighty people were killed. Since then, it has been in near-continuous activity, building a lava dome and displaying mild explosive activity from its summit crater.

In 1975, several avalanches sent rock tumbling down its sides. Four explosions distributed ash more than ten miles in any direction. In 1996, Arenal produced regular flows of lava and explosions of gas. In May 1998, it spewed large amounts of lava and ash, prompting a red alert and road closures around the volcano. More than four hundred people were evacuated, mostly tourists or workers in tourist-supported businesses. It remained one of the more active volcanoes on Earth through 2010.

Arenal sits in what is now a Costa Rica national park, the Arenal Volcano National Park. Most of the more than eight hundred species of birds in the country have been sighted in the park. Its accessibility by road and its attraction to bird watchers makes it one of the most visited parks in Costa Rica.

Arenal isn't the only national park established around one of Costa Rica's volcanoes. Parque Nacional Volcán Poás is located less than fifty miles outside San Jose, the nation's capital, where most flights from outside the country will bring you. Since the 1820s Poás has erupted forty times. On April 9, 2017, the park restricted visitors because of toxic gases at the volcano's crater. Three days later, an explosion closed the park entirely. Ten days after that, an eruption resulted in major rock damage to park buildings. After an eighteen-month extended closure, the park reopened with limited access to the volcano observation area. To visit, travelers must make a reservation via the park website. The volcano, which has two calderas filled with sulfur lakes, erupted twice in 2019.

Exploring jungles in Central America will not guarantee clean bathrooms, a Wi-Fi connection, anyone speaking your language, or no risk of being a long way from home if your travel doesn't go as expected. But the feeling of discomfort and risk can provide remote runways, hundreds of species of trees, birds, frogs, and butterflies; stories of big cats that can take down hundred-pound prey; exotic creatures that emerge in the dark of night; and active and unpredictable volcanoes. Traveling outside your comfort zone can provide experiences that become treasured lifetime memories.

Chapter 7

TAKE RISKS

Kyushu

IN THE JOURNAL *NATURE,* Dr. Roberto Sulpizio, professor in volcanology at the University of Bari, Italy, said that prediction of when a volcano might erupt "is one of the most difficult things to do." If you want to test your willingness to face one of the great uncertainties in life, go exploring volcanoes.

The best-known active volcanoes in the United States are those in Hawaii, but you can visit an active volcano in the continental United States: Mount St. Helens in Washington State. The Mount St. Helens Visitor Center, part of the Washington State Park system, is on Washington State Highway 504, only five miles off Interstate I-5 between Portland and Seattle. The best views of the volcano are fifty miles down the road at the Johnston Ridge Observatory (Milepost 52). It sits on a ridge directly in the path of the blast zone that blew out the north side of the mountain in 1980. Visitors walk the paved trail to the top of the hill for the best views. On a clear day, sometimes you can see the crater smoking.

The observatory is named for David Johnston, a United States Geological Survey (USGS) volcanologist, and one of fifty-seven people killed in the 1980 eruption of Mount St. Helens. He planned to major in journalism in college at the University of Illinois, but after an introductory class in geology he shifted his major. He did his graduate and PhD work at the University of Washington in Seattle. The focus of his dissertation was Mount Augustine in Alaska, which erupted in 1976. Johnston had done a geophysical survey there the year before. In 1978, he joined the USGS.

Mount St. Helens had last erupted in 1857. Early in 1980, after 123 years of inactivity, earthquakes rocked the area around the mountain. Seismic activity increased in late March and a plume of ash ejected more than a mile into the air on March 27. USGS geologists and volcanologists established observation posts to measure movement on the mountain. An observation post called Coldwater II was located six miles north of the mountain. The USGS hired Harry Glicken, a graduate student at the University of California, Santa Barbara, to help monitor activity at Mount St. Helens. He was stationed at Coldwater II.

Harry Glicken monitored Mount St. Helens for two weeks in early May 1980, sheltering in a trailer at Coldwater II. After working six straight days he needed to take off to attend an interview in Mammoth, California, for his graduate work. His research advisor, David Johnston, took his position at Coldwater II on Saturday, May 17. On Sunday, May 18, at 8:32 a.m. Pacific Daylight Time, the volcano erupted.

The Coldwater II observation post reported to Vancouver, Washington, by radio. David Johnston is credited with the most succinct and accurate observation in volcanic study history. His transmitted radio message on the morning of May 18, 1980, was simply, "Vancouver, Vancouver. This is it." Those were the only and last words ever heard from him.

For more than nine hours, a plume of ash blew into the sky, reaching a height of more than fifteen miles. Ash landed in eleven US states and two Canadian provinces. David Johnston's remains were never found. Remnants of the USGS trailer at Coldwater II were discovered in 1993.

TAKE RISKS

HARRY GLICKEN WENT ON to become part of an international club of volcano chasers—those studying, filming, or simply following active volcanoes. His research took him to New Zealand, the Caribbean Islands, and Japan.

On Kyushu, the southern main island of Japan, sits the 4,450-foot Mount Unzen, a stratovolcano. In 1792, after weeks of eruptions and lava flows, the collapse of a dome of the volcano created a landslide into the Ariake Sea, triggering a tsunami that killed more than 14,000 people. The volcano then remained inactive until the 1960s.

In November 1990, a steam blast eruption took place, followed by tremors and ash eruptions in mid-January and mid-February 1991. In May, lava emerged as a dome in the volcano's crater. The slow rate of extrusion of the lava and the small size of the dome that grew made the volcano seem temporarily less explosive.

Harry Glicken, then thirty-three years old, held a post at Tokyo Metropolitan University. He headed for Mount Unzen on June 2 as part of a group climbing the volcano the next day. The group included sixteen members of the press, twelve firefighters, four taxi drivers, and Maurice and Katia Krafft. They were a French couple, well known for their photography and filming of active volcanoes around the world, their life story told in a National Geographic documentary film entitled *Fire of Love*. On the afternoon of June 3, a pyroclastic flow of superheated gas and ash erupted down the mountain for more than three miles at a speed of 125 miles per hour. The gases from such a flow can reach temperatures more than 1,500°F. Harry Glicken, the Kraffts, and everyone with them were killed.

David Johnston and Harry Glicken gave their lives to not only face one of the great uncertainties of our world, but to study them. They are the only American volcanologists to have died in volcanic eruptions.

THE ADVENTURE TRAVELER'S MINDSET

ALSO ON KYUSHU IS the Sakurajima volcano. The 3,600-foot volcano sits in a bay of the East China Sea. Research indicates it erupted as early as twenty-two thousand years ago. The volcano had been inactive for a century before erupting in January 1914, the most powerful volcanic eruption in Japan in the twentieth century. The eruption and associated pyroclastic flows and earthquakes killed fifty people.

I once was invited to be one of two Anglos to speak at a conference in Tokyo, Japan. The other was film director George Casey. George had done *The Eruption of Mt. St. Helens* film, which was nominated for an Academy Award for Best Short Documentary. Prior to the meeting in Tokyo, George invited me to join him following the conference on Kyushu. He was going to visit a volcano observatory and meet the top scientist there. I accepted the invitation without giving it much thought. When we arrived, I realized the volcano observatory was built at the site of an active volcano: Sakurajima.

George Casey took me to Sakurajima to propose his idea to do a full-scale IMAX film about the "Ring of Fire," the rim of the Pacific Ocean around which most of the Earth's seismic events happen. We had rented a car to drive the road that rings around the Sakurajima volcano. We stopped at various points to take some pictures. At our first stop the ground began to shake and Sakurajima erupted. Ash went a half mile into the sky. We were rendered mute. We were downwind and I found myself grinding ash between my teeth. Back in the car we went.

This was not the only eruption of Sakurajima in the few days we were there. Sakurajima has been in a continuous state of eruption since 1955, typically explosive blasts of ash. Hundreds happen each year, with ash columns rising thousands of feet high. An ash plume eruption on August 18, 2013, reached a height of three miles. It was the five hundreth ash eruption that year.

TAKE RISKS

Two and a half miles across the bay from the volcano is Kagoshima, a city with 600,000 residents. Kagoshima is a sister city of Naples, Italy, which sits five miles from Mount Vesuvius. Vesuvius erupted in the year 79 AD, burying the city of Pompeii.

In Kagoshima, residents manage ash falls like those in winter climates manage snow falls. We spent our time at Sakurajima staying at the Sun Royal Hotel. We stayed in rooms on the volcano side of the hotel. You can sit outside on your balcony with a great view of Sakurajima. I awoke one night in a jet-lagged state and wandered onto my balcony. It was just before sunrise and the volcano was silhouetted smoking against the first light of the day. I sat on my balcony alone in the dawn light. The view seduced me into the idea of doing a film about the Ring of Fire.

A ferry carries vehicles and pedestrians between Kagoshima and Sakurajima. There is a shop on the ferry that serves udon noodle soup. Udon is a thick wheat flour noodle served in hot soup, topped with chopped scallions and often a thin slice of fishcake. On the first morning we took the ferry from Kagoshima, we ordered udon soup and sat outside at the front of the boat. To this day I believe it was the best udon noodle soup I ever had in Japan—probably because I was sailing into an active volcano that just loomed larger and larger during the twenty-minute ferry trip from Kagoshima.

More than five thousand people live around the base of the volcano, many of whom farm the area's rich soil laid down from thousands of years of eruptions. The island is known for the volleyball-sized white radishes that grow there. It is said that the volcanic ash in the soil creates optimal growing conditions. Every year, the residents of Sakurajima hold a volcano disaster drill on January 11, the anniversary of the 1914 eruption. School children wearing hard hats march onto ferries, along with senior citizens who come for the lunch provided on the day of the disaster.

One of the biggest risks at Sakurajima, and many volcanoes worldwide, is ash spewing down mountain river valleys. The river water and ash become a slurry, like a wet cement rushing down a hillside. At Sakurajima, the natural valleys down the side of the mountain have been made into concrete spillways to help direct heavy, wet ash flows. Shelters, essentially concrete bunkers, have been built along the roadway that circles the volcano.

I WENT BACK TO Minnesota and presented the plan for a Ring of Fire film to the museum's board of trustees. They agreed to it. We would develop a SWAT squad to chase volcanic events. SWAT stands for "special weapons and tactics," a term historically used for an at-the-ready specialized force of military personnel, equipment, and tactics. Our squad would be based out of Los Angeles, and they would be ready at a moment's notice to fly off to the Pacific Basin with an IMAX camera to record activity, or the aftermath, of volcanoes and earthquakes. Our plan was to dedicate three years to chasing volcanoes and capturing action footage of actual eruptions. Then we would go and film at locations where activity was more predictable and document the diverse stories of the people and cultures of the Pacific Rim.

We were hardwired into the Smithsonian Institution's Global Volcanism Program, which provides constant monitoring of worldwide volcanic activity and quick dissemination of eruption reports. From it we learned that the Rabaul Volcano in Papua New Guinea had become seismically active. It had last erupted in 1937. Since that time, a town had developed inside the inactive caldera, the cone of the volcano. Our SWAT squad jetted off to Rabaul and began filming from both the ground and the air. We imagined we'd have incredible establishing shots of people living *in* the volcano, followed by a devastating eruption. Alas, the volcano went quiet.

As we neared the end of the three-year period that we dedicated to capturing erupting volcano action footage, we had none. I dreaded the thought of reporting to the board of trustees that I had spent a lot of money but didn't have anything to show for it. I went to bed each night knowing it could be the end of my career at the museum. My IMAX film days and life of adventure travel would be over. It was time not to surrender to such possibilities. It was time to embrace another inevitable uncertainty of life. It was time to keep moving forward.

Then, on Christmas Day 1988, the Lonquimay Volcano in Chile's Andes Mountains erupted for the first time in fifty years. The eruption began with ejections of gas and water vapor. The next day, gas and ash rose thousands of feet into the air, lava began to flow, and an explosion of material rose five miles within minutes. Our film team had been monitoring Lonquimay, as the region had become seismically active earlier in the year.

On Christmas Eve, there had been a tremor felt sixty miles away. Our film team headed from southern California to Chile right away. Our principal cinematographer couldn't get into Chile because he held an Iranian passport, but the rest of the team arrived in time to film days' worth of footage before the volcano calmed on January 6. The crew captured fragments as large as cars being blasted from the volcano and crashing on the nearby landscape—all on IMAX film. The film crew slept in tents on the isolated landscape of the 9,400-foot volcano as it provided nightly explosions.

There was no bad weather, no rain or snow, or cloudy days—only the erupting volcano for our crew at Lonquimay. The symmetrical stratovolcano proved to be photogenic amidst the scenery of the Andes Mountains of Chile. It was the hoped-for positive turn of our luck for filming tectonic activity in the Pacific region.

Ten months after documenting the Lonquimay eruption,

our film team had returned from filming in Indonesia. Before they finished unpacking their gear in Los Angeles, an earthquake happened in San Francisco. It was October 17, and the third game of the World Series was scheduled to take place in Candlestick Park. The pre-game TV broadcast had only begun when the earthquake hit at 5:04 p.m. local time. Our film crew was on location at sunrise the next day to begin filming in the aftermath of the earthquake that collapsed the Cypress Freeway in Oakland and did major damage in San Francisco's Marina District and throughout the region. More than ten thousand homes and two thousand businesses sustained damage.

Our patience, dedication of time, and taking the risk of going to volcanoes to film the unpredictability of their eruptions, ultimately paid off. After seven years of chasing volcanoes and earthquakes around the Pacific Basin, the *Ring of Fire* IMAX film was successfully completed. It went on to show in thirty-five countries, in more than 150 cities, and in sixteen different languages.

Chapter 8

EMBRACE FAMILIARITY

Hong Kong

MY FIRST TRIP TO Hong Kong marked the first time I had flown on an airplane for more than four hours. When I took off from Minneapolis, it was already thirteen hours later—*tomorrow*—in Hong Kong. I lost track of what time it was or where I was. The flight was about sixteen hours. It resulted in jet lag, which can put a traveler out of sorts and add to a traveler's uneasiness. This trip taught me to not complain about jet lag, but to relish it. Jet lag means you are fortunate to have been transported quickly a long way from home. At the same time, jet lag informs a traveler to prioritize self-care. I made sure to stay hydrated and to get enough sleep before and during the long-distance flight. This helped mitigate the anxiousness and agitation I felt from going through multiple time zones and into new surroundings. I also followed long-held advice for travel to new and distant places. I made sure to eat light and eat right, to minimize alcohol intake, to take walks, and to slow down.

KAI TAK AIRPORT WAS Hong Kong's international airport at the time of my trip. The airport operated until 1998, when it was replaced with a new airport built twenty miles to the west. The History Channel's *Most Extreme Airports* ranked Kai Tak as the sixth most dangerous in the world. Landing on a runway surrounded by water on three sides required a forty-five degree turn when the airplane was less than six hundred feet high. This approach earned it the nickname "Kai Tak Heart Attack."

Kai Tak has a long and interesting history. It was a small grass strip runway operated for a flying school and aviation club in the 1920s. The first hangar and control tower were built in 1935. The Japanese took over Hong Kong during World War II and used prisoner-of-war labor to build two concrete runways. The airport was modernized in the 1950s, expanding the two runways to 5,500 and 4,700 feet in length. There were no operations at night. In 1958, a new 8,000-foot runway was built into Victoria Harbor. It was extended in the 1970s to 11,130 feet, its final length through the end of the airport's operation. In 1996, Kai Tak handled thirty million passengers.

I'll never forget the descent into Hong Kong on my first flight there. In the deep darkness of the South China Sea, the first lights I saw were on boats in the harbor. Then the lights appeared on Hong Kong Island, which rose out of the darkness of the water to 1,800 feet high. Sitting on the left side of the plane I felt like the Boeing 747 Jumbo Jet was going to land on the water. From where I was sitting, I couldn't see the runway on the approach for landing—only the water getting closer and closer in the darkness.

My trip started the day after Thanksgiving in the United States. The Christmas season had begun, and in Hong Kong there were decorations with Santa in his sleigh pulled by his team of reindeer. This even though the residents of Hong Kong had no experience with winter or snow.

On a shopping trip, I bought a half dozen little decorated Chinese silk purses. The vendor asked if I had a lot of girlfriends. I said no, they were for my many female cousins in Seattle, where I would be visiting after traveling in the Orient. I told him my aunt and uncle had a lot of kids as they were a Catholic family.

He looked puzzled. "Is that the one with the cross?" he asked. This was the only reference to Christianity I experienced during my time in Hong Kong. None of their Christmas decorations included any reference to, or images of, the baby Jesus, Mary, or Joseph. No wise men. No shepherds.

HONG KONG IS A peninsula jutting into the South China Sea. Off the tip of the peninsula is Hong Kong Island. Between the peninsula and the island is Victoria Harbor, a deep harbor that accommodates large trading ships—the same ships that advanced the development of Hong Kong. The highest point on the island is Victoria Peak. "The Peak" has surrounding parks with hiking trails, along with a highly valued residential area. It features spectacular views of the island's dense business district, the peninsula beyond, and Victoria Harbor. A trip on the tram to the top of the island is a must-do on a visit. The night views from The Peak are indelible.

My first trip to Hong Kong included a bus ride around to the south side of the island, where the most expensive real estate in the world is located. It also included a stop at the beach at Repulse Bay. In late November, the beach was out of season for locals. But I had come from Minnesota to this semitropical environment 22° north of the equator. I welcomed the beach day with its beautiful ocean breeze and views of Hong Kong's smaller islands.

Repulse Bay is one of those geographic names with no definitive origins; myriad myths surround it. One is that the bay was used by pirates in the 1840s, which disrupted merchant ships trading with China. The British Royal Navy repulsed the pirates and thus gave the bay its name.

THE ADVENTURE TRAVELER'S MINDSET

HONG KONG ISLAND IS thirty square miles—a fraction of Hong Kong's total area. You can reach the mainland by car through tunnels like the Cross-Harbor Tunnel, which was built in the 1970s. You can also take the subway. However, the best way across Victoria Harbor is to take the Star Ferry. The white and green ferries are a symbol of Hong Kong.

The Star Ferry's upper deck is its first-class section, but it is too sterile to recommend. I suggest a ride on the lower deck, the "ordinary class," where you will find better views, no glass covering the windows, and an opportunity to share the ride with the locals. The harbor traffic includes barges, Russian cruise liners, fishing boats, tugboats and sampans. I found myself riding back and forth on multiple occasions on all my trips to Hong Kong. My rides on the ferry always gave me an exhilarating feeling of being very far from where my journey started.

A short walk from the Star Ferry dock at the tip of Kowloon Peninsula is Ocean Terminal. The large pier is marketed as Harbor City, with an emphasis on shopping at its more than one hundred stores. A bit hidden away on the second story of Ocean Terminal, you will find the entrance to the restaurant Dan Ryan's.

ONE EVENING, I FOUND myself in a hotel basement bar sitting next to a chap with an English accent. I surrendered to the moment and listened to his story. He said he was part of a group of a dozen people who saw an opportunity for "themed" restaurants in this part of the world. They decided they wanted an American-themed restaurant in Hong Kong, and they thought an American city theme would do the trick. They rejected New York as too obvious and settled on Chicago, even though none of the restaurant developers were from there. They also recognized it for its legacy as a commercial meatpacking industry

EMBRACE FAMILIARITY

center, which inspired the menu at Dan Ryan's, their new Hong Kong restaurant.

Daniel B. Ryan, Jr.—Dan Ryan—was a member of the Cook County Board of Commissioners, starting in 1930. He served on the Roads and Bridges Committee. He proposed that an auto expressway be built through the city of Chicago in Cook County. He was the president of the board from 1954 until his death in 1961 at age sixty-six. As president, he moved forward bond funding for the highway. Eighteen months after his death, the stretch of expressway through the south side of Chicago opened. It was named the Dan Ryan.

When I hung out at Dan Ryan's at Ocean Terminal, it had a bar that was three sided, like a U with flat sides and a half dozen seats on each side. I learned that if you took a seat at the center of the base of the U, you could carry on a conversation with anyone at the bar. Everyone who came to the bar when I was there was an internationalist. I met ex-pats from the United Kingdom, American kickboxers on their return home from an international competition in China, and tourists and traders from all over the world. The bar at Dan Ryan's exemplifies, and magnifies, what makes Hong Kong such an extraordinary place. It also has a Midwest American menu that includes a BBQ chicken and pork ribs combo platter, which are hard to find in Asia. I welcomed such fare anytime I spent a few weeks traveling and dining in this part of the world.

Self-care during long-distance travel involves more than tending to physical needs. Emotional, social, and spiritual self-care are additional considerations. One emotional self-care tip is to give yourself a win—plan something to look forward to. For me, on my trips to this part of the world, I always finished my travels by visiting Hong Kong and spending time at Dan Ryan's—my favorite bar in the world.

As a native Chicago south-sider, I found myself in Hong

Kong one Sunday morning at Dan Ryan's as it was opening. I took my place at my favorite seat at the bar. The restaurant was not yet serving food, and the bar was empty, so I took my drink and walked around, looking at all the Chicago memorabilia—mostly black-and-white photos on the walls. I commented on one of the photos to a Chinese waitress who was setting a table near me. As I walked alongside the wall, providing her a tutorial on the history encapsulated in the wall decorations, I turned around and saw there were now a half dozen waitresses, all Chinese, listening to my ruminations about my home city. No one had ever told them about the real and rare connection their restaurant had to a city thirteen time zones away.

THROUGH 2006 AND 2007, the Illinois Department of Transportation reconstructed the entire length of the Dan Ryan in the largest expressway reconstruction project in Chicago history. It cost $975,000,000, almost twice the original cost estimate. Tourist guides for Asia will say that Dan Ryan's in Hong Kong is named after a Chicago expressway, failing to note the expressway was named after a Chicago politician. In 2018, Bill Daley, the youngest child of former Chicago south-sider Mayor Richard Daley, proposed renaming the Dan Ryan expressway. Bill proposed renaming the expressway after his former boss, for whom he served as White House chief of staff. That boss was another Chicago south-sider—Barack Obama. However, after many decades, the expressway running through the south side of Chicago, and the restaurant and bar at Ocean Terminal in Hong Kong, are still named after Dan Ryan.

Chapter 9

ADOPT A ROAD WARRIOR

Greenland

ONE OF THE GREATEST road warriors I ever traveled with was our film distribution manager, Mike Boeckmann. He embodied the road warrior mentality: he blended into his immediate environment with ease. He remained calm during challenging travel circumstances. He bonded with new people like they were old friends and at the start of a trip he could talk his way into airport lounges. He could be entrusted to go anywhere.

One of the greatest ways to travel is to do it with a road warrior like Mike. Your travel will be less stressful and more enhanced if you can identify and go with such a person. While I continue to learn the skills to address the uncertainty, unpredictability, and anxiety that comes with travel, road warriors seem to live all the lessons without even thinking about them. If you are lucky, you may uncover a road warrior within your extended family. If so, take them with you on your travels. I was fortunate enough to have worked with a couple of people that I would describe as true travel ninjas.

When we decided to do an IMAX film about the greatest places on earth, we had a full list of locations to scout. Mike and I divided the list to ensure one or the other of us would be part of every scouting trip. I chose to go to the Namib Desert and the

THE ADVENTURE TRAVELER'S MINDSET

Okavango Delta. Without hesitation, he chose one of the more challenging places to visit: Greenland.

FOR MOST OF HUMAN history, Greenland has been settled sparsely by arctic indigenous peoples, the Inuit, who probably migrated there through northern Canada. The Vikings, who named it, settled there for a while. Afflicted by malnutrition, a pandemic, and a decline in temperatures called the Little Ice Age, they couldn't make a go of it.

Greenland runs 1,800 miles north to south, and it is 680 miles across at its widest point. It is more than three times the size of Texas, though the population of Texas is almost five hundred times that of Greenland. Most of Greenland lies north of the Arctic Circle and almost all its population lives along the southwest coast. An ice sheet, the largest in the northern hemisphere, covers most of the rest of the island. On more than one occasion, the United States has offered to buy Greenland, but Denmark claims it and refuses to sell. Greenland is closer to the North Pole than it is to Copenhagen. The population of indigenous people outnumber the Danes in Greenland almost ten to one.

The towns on the island of Greenland have no roads to connect them. Travel between them is mainly by boat, as well as by plane, snowmobile, and dogsled.

IN 1882, TWENTY-YEAR-OLD FRIDTJOF Nansen, a native Norwegian, arrived on the east coast of Greenland on a sealing ship. Two years earlier, he had entered university to study zoology, believing it would provide him the opportunity to work outside. The head of his college zoology department encouraged him to join a five-month voyage to Greenland to study the

Arctic environment. The trip began in mid-March. In July the expedition became temporarily stranded in the ice off the coast of Greenland. Nansen became mesmerized with the idea of crossing the island.

No explorer had ever reached the center of the ice sheet, let alone crossed Greenland entirely. A previous expedition led by Robert Peary in 1886, twenty-three years before he claimed to have reached the north pole, had set out from the west coast of Greenland and traveled one hundred miles toward the interior before turning back.

Nansen's plan had three unique ideas. First, he proposed crossing east to west, from the isolated to the inhabited side. Previous uncompleted expeditions had begun on the west coast, where the settlements were. Second, Nansen carefully recruited a much smaller crew than previous expeditions. Six men, including himself, would make up the team, all adept skiers with extreme outdoor experience. His third daring idea? To cross Greenland on skis.

As with previous expeditions, the team considered using dogs or reindeer to pull the sleds, but that added the challenge—and weight—of feeding animals. Trying different cookers and fuels, wooden skis, and sleds, he settled on what he regarded as the best option for success. The Nansen team members themselves would pull the sleds loaded with provisions and gear.

They planned to launch from a sealing ship in June 1888, taking small boats through the expected ice packs to the coast. In mid-June, their ship became locked in the ice for ten days. On July 14, they were thirty-five miles from shore. On July 17, when they were twelve miles from the coast, the team got into two boats and began rowing. One of the boats began taking on water after being pierced by ice. They pulled the boat onto an ice floe to patch over the leak. It began raining hard, so they set up a tent to spend the night.

Pack ice moves. The team awoke farther south than they started, and ten miles farther from shore. They spent a second night, waking up thirty miles from shore. On the fourth night, the current carried the ice floe closer. They finally arrived on the island of Greenland eleven days after they started.

Two days after the start of the team's trek west across Greenland, a windstorm with driving rain confined them to their tents for three days. Near the end of August, they changed course, shortening their planned 350-mile trek by almost one hundred miles. In mid-September, they had reached their highest altitude of almost nine-thousand feet above sea level. It was -35°F, but they were now headed down the slope toward the west coast. Upon arriving on the coast in late September, they were far south of any settlement. They reconfigured their sleds and tents, fashioning a boat to head up the coast. For much of the way, they pulled their boat as they hiked through coastal muck. On October 3, a Danish official met them to let them know people had been watching for their arrival all along the coast. The crossing had taken forty-nine days.

Eager to get home, the crew asked about boats leaving Greenland and heading back to Europe. They learned that the last boat for the year had left Greenland two months ago. They spent the winter in Greenland before returning to Norway in May 1889.

AS A TEENAGER, GERMAN Alfred Wegener had read of Nansen's exploits in Greenland. In 1906, Wegener participated in what was called the Denmark expedition, the first of his four Greenland expeditions. During the Denmark expedition he constructed the first true meteorological station in Greenland. Three members of the expedition starved to death after being stranded on a side trip to the north coast.

ADOPT A ROAD WARRIOR

In 1913 Wegener was part of an expedition that crossed Greenland via a route through the center of the island. The route was twice as long as Nansen's 1888 expedition across southern Greenland. In July 1930, Wegener along with four Greenlanders, and a former student, German scientist Johannes Georgi, traveled 250 miles and to an altitude of 9,850 feet to set up a science station in the middle of Greenland. The team unloaded the gear, set up a weather station and a tent, and then, as was planned, left Georgi alone. It was 17°F. They left a string of black flags on tall stakes along a track toward the west coast.

On his second day alone, Georgi decided to dig out a small room under the ice to protect his instruments from wild temperature swings. He not only dug a room in the ice, but he also cut out ice blocks and built a wall around the top of a stairway leading down to his room. He expected sled teams to resupply him before winter.

One sled arrived on September 13 with three thousand pounds of provisions and fuel. Glaciologist Ernst Sorge, who was thirty-one years old and ten years younger than Georgi, stayed on. They divided their scientific efforts. "The snow line was the line of demarcation," Sorge wrote in his journal. Everything above the snow—the meteorological work—was done by Georgi. Everything below the ice was the research done by Sorge.

Georgi and Sorge dug deeper to measure ice thickness, and eventually began living below ground because it was more comfortable than their shelter near the surface. They descended steps behind a door of fur to a cavern six feet below. "Our impression was that we were lying in state in a crypt, everything clean cut and rectangular, white like marble," Sorge wrote.

If they didn't get a final shipment of provisions by October 20, Georgi and Sorge planned to walk back to the west coast.

The resupply never came. They decided they could manage winter with the provisions they had.

On October 30, they heard voices. It was Wegener, who had led a group on a 250-mile journey from the west coast on September 21. The trip was expected to take sixteen days; it ended up taking forty. Fifteen people had been part of the group at the outset, but twelve turned around when they reached the one hundred–mile mark from their starting point, fearful of making the trip out and back safely. Wegener was afraid that Georgi and Sorge would be heading back from their camp as planned on October 20. If that had been the case, it appeared to be a matter of life-and-death for him to find them.

Wegener and one member of his party then headed back toward the west coast on November 1. The other member, meteorologist Fritz Loewe, had frostbitten feet and was unable to walk. He stayed with Georgi and Sorge. Wegener's return trip was late in the season, but they would be traveling downhill on the ice sheet, and they expected to have the wind at their backs.

Gangrene had set in on Loewe's frozen toes and he was in terrible pain. Georgi and Sorge decided to amputate his toes. They had no surgical instruments. They did have a pocketknife and metal cutting shears. They amputated all the toes on Loewe's right foot and three on his left. Slowly, his feet began to heal. Weeks later, he began to hobble around.

Since those on the coast had no way to communicate with the Georgi camp in the middle of the island, they thought Wegener and his companion had decided to spend the winter with Georgi, Sorge, and Loewe.

The first spring resupply from the west coast came on May 7. Upon arrival that team realized, along with Georgi's three-man mid-ice team, that Wegener and his companion were gone. At mile 118, halfway between the west coast and the science camp at the center of Greenland, they found Wegener's skis planted upright in the snow. It was there they found his body. His companion was never found.

Fridtjof Nansen's drive to explore Greenland was not only an idea for adventure. Nansen's crossing of Greenland involved recording temperature, wind, and precipitation where it had never been recorded. He was a scientist who wrote, "Every single section of the Earth's surface stands in intimate and reciprocal relation to its neighbors," and that Greenland's "tract of ice and snow must have an as yet unmeasured influence on the climate."

IN 1993, AFTER FIVE years of drilling, the US National Science Foundation penetrated through the ice sheet to the bedrock below. The ice core they recovered was almost two miles in depth. It reveals a weather history of the planet of more than one hundred thousand years. It indicates that the Greenland ice sheet is melting at the fastest rate since the end of the last ice age, twelve thousand years ago.

The melting of Greenland's ice sheet will not only result in rising sea levels that will affect low-lying and coastal communities thousands of miles away, but also has the potential, in combination with melting polar sea ice, for it to impact Atlantic Ocean circulation. This circulation is one system of currents that includes the Florida Current and the Gulf Stream, which influence the climate in North America and Europe. The distribution of temperature variance in the oceans is what has kept Europe relatively warm despite its northern latitudes. Glasgow, Scotland, is 2° of latitude farther north than Edmonton, Alberta, but its average January high temperature is 20°F warmer.

As warm tropical water circulates northward, it becomes cooler and denser. Ice melting from Greenland adds more fresh water to the system, making the water less salty and less dense, which disrupts the circulation. And so Greenland, sparsely populated, rarely visited, and rarely referenced in human history, is a key driver of the planet's climate, which will affect all of humanity.

We know why Greenland is melting. Human activity has added carbon to the atmosphere at a rate one hundred times faster than recorded for the last 500,000 years. Increased carbon in the atmosphere causes the planet's temperatures to rise. From multiple sources, including the records revealed in Antarctic ice cores and stalagmites from ancient caves, we know how much carbon dioxide (CO_2) has been in the atmosphere for the last half million years.

The amount of CO_2 in the atmosphere is measured in parts per million (PPM). Since the last ice age, through all written human history, CO_2 has varied little from 280 PPM. Since the start of the industrial age, we have added more than 140 PPM. Most of that carbon was added since 1990. As of 2020, human activity has increased the amount of carbon in the atmosphere to more than 420 PPM.

Greenland is a big cog in the global climate wheel. Its ice sheet rises from the coasts to an altitude of nine thousand feet and covers more than 80 percent of the island. During the summer, ice will melt on its surface. The warming climate has led to more days of melting ice in recent years, along with larger areas of melting. In 2012, more than 90 percent of the ice sheet experienced melting at the surface. In April 2016, Greenland saw its earliest melt days ever recorded in any previous year. When the entire ice sheet melts, it will raise sea levels by twenty-four feet.

ONE OF THE MORE interesting stories our film distribution manager Mike came back with from his film scouting trip was of boating with a Greenlander. Moving between icebergs, the Greenlander shot a seal with a rifle. He butchered it on shore on a stainless steel table. People appeared with plastic bags to fill with seal meat. The Greenlander had a scale to weigh the bags and quickly sold out the entire inventory by weight.

One evening Mike hiked up a high ridge to a vista of the Ilulissat Icefjord, a glacier moving out of a deep and long valley on the west side of Greenland near the town of Ilulissat. The glacier's rate of movement varies from year to year and has been measured moving down the valley at a rate of 150 feet per day. It is estimated to contribute to 10 percent of the icebergs that calve into the North Atlantic Ocean, one of which was the iceberg that sank the Titanic. Mike said when he climbed to the top of a rise overlooking the glacier, he looked more than five miles up the valley and "couldn't digest the beauty of it." He said it brought him to tears.

I regard true road warriors as more than individuals who navigate their way on distant travel with the ease of being at home. They are travelers who view and respect magnificent works of nature like works of fine art. They allow themselves to shed a tear in the face of nature's spectacles.

Chapter 10

PRACTICE MINDFULNESS

Tanzania

A MOMENT WHEN I practiced mindfulness led me from Valencia, Spain, to the shore of Lake Tanganyika in Tanzania. This happened for me while I attended a conference in Valencia during the Falles Festival. My hosts from the Ciudad de las Artes y las Ciencias, the City of Arts and Sciences, took a group of us to an event traditionally held in conjunction with the annual festival: the bullfights.

The bulls are reared on breeding estates and raised specifically for bullfights. They reach more than 1,200 pounds in weight. A fight culminates with a bull incited to charge by the waving of a red cape by a matador. A series of such passes is a highlight of the event, especially when the bull passes dangerously close to the bullfighter. The matador then uses the cape to maneuver the bull into a position for the matador to use a sword to stab it between the shoulder blades.

As anticipated, the bulls lost every fight. At the end of each fight, a team of horses came out and dragged the dead bull out of the arena, leaving a bloodied track across the dirt surface. The ground crew would then come out and rake the arena in preparation for the next fight. After the first bloody finish, many of my colleagues who, like myself, were attending their first bullfight, felt they had seen more than enough and left. I found it a moment for mindfulness.

Mindfulness has Buddhist roots and is a practice of bringing your mind to a place where it can rest and settle. Mindfulness supports being aware of where you are, and not to overly react to what is going on. Mindfulness asks us to suspend immediate judgement and unlock our curiosity. I took a deep breath, suspended my own judgement, and waited for the entrance of the next bull.

As it turns out, my not following my colleagues out of the bullfight resulted in one of the best film projects I was ever involved with. As the group I came with thinned out, I got engaged in a conversation with a colleague, Jim Marchbank, who also remained at the bullfight, a colleague I had never met. He was the head of the science center in Sudbury, Ontario. Sudbury is the site of the world's largest nickel mine, which supports the economic operation of the cultural facility. The Valencia gathering was a mid-winter meeting of worldwide museums operating IMAX theaters, and Sudbury was planning on building such a theater and making films for it.

The Sudbury museum did build a theater, and after it opened, my colleague called me to say that Dr. Jane Goodall had visited his museum and watched an IMAX film. I asked what film she saw and what she thought. He said she saw the film *Mountain Gorillas*. Her comment: "Great format. Wrong primate."

Marchbank asked if I thought we could put together the financing and a team to do an IMAX film about Dr. Goodall. I had already served as an executive producer for several films, and that initial conversation led to a discussion about numerous avenues for support on both sides of the border. The idea for the film was also supported by the fact that at that time the University of Minnesota in the Twin Cities housed all the field notes by Dr. Goodall—notes recorded at her study site for more than four decades.

JANE GOODALL'S FATHER DIDN'T give his young daughter a teddy bear. He gave her a stuffed chimpanzee. When she was in her mid-twenties, still filled with her childhood love of animals, she migrated from her home in England to the farm of a friend in Kenya. This friend encouraged her to give a call to famed archaeologist Dr. Louis Leakey. He and his co-researcher and spouse, British paleoanthropologist Mary Leakey, hired Goodall as a secretary and sent her to Olduvai Gorge in Tanzania.

In July 1960, with funding secured by Louis Leakey, Goodall went to what was later to become the Gombe Stream Research Centre on the eastern shore of Lake Tanganyika. Gombe is only accessible by boat and is home to scores of bird species and several primate species including vervet monkeys, baboons, and chimpanzees. The chief warden of Gombe was concerned about the safety of a young woman coming to live there. He approved her assignment when he learned her mother would come along.

In animal studies, it is standard practice to give subjects numbers. Instead, Goodall gave the chimpanzees names. She established a naming convention where newborn chimps received a name that started with the same letter as their mother's name. "It was not permissible to talk about an animal's mind," she once wrote. "Only humans had minds." But in studying, writing about, and living with chimpanzees, Jane determined, "It isn't only human beings who have personality, who are capable of rational thought and emotions like joy and sorrow." The work of Goodall and her associates over many decades has taught us that, with respect to chimpanzees, "close, supportive, affectionate bonds develop between family members and other individuals within a community that can persist through a life span of more than fifty years."

Chimpanzees live in communities of twenty to one hundred individuals covering a geographic area. Like we humans, theirs is a fission-fusion society, meaning that in any given day, we come together in group settings and also spend time alone. Chimpanzees reach their sexual maturity in their teens. Females typically give birth every few years, almost always to a single offspring, though twins have been born at Gombe. Mothers rear their infants. Infants also have relationships with close females and older siblings. Young chimps are weaned at about the age of five and, until their teen years, remain close to their mothers. Most female chimps will only have three or four young in their lifetime. Chimpanzee social groups consist of adult females, young chimps, and adult males, including a dominant male—the alpha male. As young males reach maturity, they might challenge their leader to establish social dominance.

Chimpanzees have complex daily lives. They groom each other. They learn from each other. They hug each other. They chase, play, and tickle each other. They swagger. They vocalize in a mixture of grunts, barks, and pant-hoots, which are distinct to each individual. They will also communicate nonverbally, with gestures, postures, and facial expressions. At the end of daylight, adult chimpanzees make "night nests" in the trees to sleep in. They build new nests each night, which results in less accumulation of bacteria, or bed bugs, than might be found in human beds.

BEFORE HUMAN SETTLEMENT IN this part of Africa, forested hillsides spanned the length of the eastern shore of Lake Tanganyika, the world's longest freshwater lake—all habitat for chimpanzee communities. Today, Gombe is like an island of the original habitat. It runs four miles along the lakeshore. The hillside of the park rises steeply from the shoreline up a half mile high. Numerous steep-sided stream valleys run down the hillside. A hiker going up from the beach will find open woodland of semideciduous and evergreen forests, giving way to a grass-topped ridge that marks the top of the park. Gombe, home to three chimpanzee communities, has no roads to it or through it. Goodall's study group has been the central community, the Kasekela community.

On November 4, 1960, Jane Goodall made and sketched an observation unrecognized by the world of science. Up until that point, researchers believed that only humans could construct and use tools. On that day, Goodall watched a chimpanzee at a termite mound take twigs from trees, remove the leaves, and poke them into holes in the mound. When the chimpanzee removed the twigs from the mound, they were covered with clinging termites. The chimp would then feed off the twigs. Effectively, the chimpanzee had selected a proper pole to "fish" for termites.

Dr. Goodall also observed that chimpanzees had an aggressive nature. "During the first ten years of the study I believed that the chimpanzees were rather nicer than human beings," she said. "Then we found they could be brutal—that they had, like us, a darker side to their nature." They will hunt and eat smaller primates like colobus monkeys. And Goodall observed dominant females killing and even cannibalizing the young of other females.

The male population of a community will patrol their community borders—silently and in single file. The hierarchy, dominated by an alpha male, is suspended as the chimpanzees line up by age, with the oldest toward the front of the patrol. They sniff the ground. They stop. They listen. They are on the lookout for chimps from neighboring communities. If they encounter males, a violent fight will result. They bite, kick, and hit. The encounter may result in the expansion of their territory, or it might bring new females into their group.

The Gombe Chimpanzee War took place between 1974 and 1978, when the Kasekela community split. The separatists were six or seven adult males, along with three females and their young. Eight adult males, twelve adult females, and their young made up the remaining community. After the four-year conflict, the splinter group was eventually eliminated.

WHILE THE IDEA OF doing an IMAX film about Jane Goodall stimulated our appetite to rush forward, it was important to practice mindfulness in our approach. We didn't want to go with immediate ideas when developing a storyline. Front-end evaluation became the proper starting point for the opportunity, including understanding what our audiences would expect and what their knowledge and curiosity about Jane Goodall's story was.

We held discussion groups with audiences that had attended films in our museums. The sessions began with a warmup, where we asked people to introduce themselves and name their favorite film they had seen in our theater. We asked them to write down the names of famous woman scientists, along with answers to a few other prompting questions. We were delighted when we went around the table and heard many respondents with Dr. Goodall on their list. Often, hers was the only name on a list. We learned that our participants had general knowledge about her primate studies in Africa, but they didn't know what had happened to her or her study subjects, or even if Dr. Goodall was still living. We recognized our opportunity was to tell the updated story of Dr. Goodall and the new generation of researchers carrying on her work in Gombe.

In 1977, the Jane Goodall Institute was established to

protect chimpanzees and their habitat and support the research Goodall started. The proper starting point to share our formative research about potential film storylines was to meet with Dr. Goodall and representatives of her Institute. Jane Goodall Institute operations were established in multiple countries, including in Canada with headquarters in Montreal. In October 1997, Jim Marchbank and I got on the agenda for a Saturday meeting of the board of directors of the Jane Goodall Institute of Canada. Dr. Goodall would be in attendance. We had thirty minutes to make our pitch to produce an IMAX film about Jane and the chimpanzees of Gombe.

We were on the agenda for mid-morning, and when we arrived at the Institute offices the executive director stepped out of the conference room where the board was meeting. She told us the meeting was already running behind schedule and asked if we could stay past our scheduled time. I had flown in from Minneapolis the day before and had dedicated the entire day to ensure we had flexibility to meet any last-minute schedule changes. Having already come this far, we were not going to say no to hanging around.

While we waited in the reception area to be called into the meeting, I looked to see where Dr. Goodall was sitting in the room. She was at the head of the table nearest the doorway. After half an hour the executive director came out and said they were going to take their first break of the morning. She asked if we could help carry in a couple of chairs for our allotted time. I set my chair right next to Dr. Goodall's. I figured if our idea did not meet with a warm reception, at least I would have a half hour sitting next to her.

We talked through our idea, shared our research, and passed out materials we had brought. I had a video of *Ring of Fire*, a giant screen film on which I had been executive producer. My film crews and I had spent seven years chasing volcanoes around the

Pacific Basin to make the film, so it was a good representation as to the seriousness of our experience and commitment to making an IMAX film. Dr. Goodall seemed disinterested during our pitch. She held the video box for *Ring of Fire* while we answered questions from board members. The back of the box featured on-location production pictures, which included Mount St. Helens. When the Institute executive director thanked us for coming and stood up to indicate our time was up, Dr. Goodall put her hand on my forearm while we were still seated. She leaned into me and said, "Mike, I carry around symbols of hope that tell the story of life's rejuvenation. I need something from Mount St. Helens that tells that story." She didn't say "please." She didn't ask, "Could you get me something?" She didn't say anything about the film.

I left the room wondering why she never said anything about our film idea. What did this mean for the project? I then reminded myself that mindfulness is awareness that arises from paying attention to the purpose of the present moment. I had the strong feeling that I had to, for now, suspend being a filmmaker. I had been selected to be a disciple for her work.

In the making of our *Ring of Fire* film, we had filmed at Mount St. Helens and had made many contacts there. The week following my meeting in Montreal, I called the plant biologist at Mount St. Helens's National Volcanic Monument. "I was with Jane Goodall over the weekend," I said. "Here is what she needs."

The biologist sent me leaves with notes about how this plant species had made a remarkable comeback after the area was buried in ash following the 1980 eruption. Since I worked in a museum, I had access to experts in collections, curation, and exhibitory. My colleagues mounted the leaves on acid-free paper and put them in a small frame with a label of information.

Staff at the University of Minnesota worked with Dr. Goodall, so they were able to provide me her travel schedule. I learned that the following month, she would be in Washington, D.C., followed by Fargo, North Dakota, the next day. There was only one way to meet that schedule, and that was to fly through MSP, the airport serving Minneapolis–Saint Paul.

This was in the days before TSA security at airports, back when you could go to an airport gate to greet someone or see them off. I got Goodall's flight schedule and walked to the gate for her flight to Fargo. I spotted her and an empty seat next to her. I sat down and, without a word, handed her what she had told me she needed when we had met the month before. She looked at it, read the label, and put her hand back on my forearm. She said, "Mike, let's talk about making that IMAX film."

In May of 1998, we headed to Jane Goodall's study site on the eastern shore of Lake Tanganyika to scout the location for production of the film. To minimize the risk of carrying the flu virus into the chimpanzee habitat, we were required to get flu shots prior to our arrival. That winter, there was a shortage of flu vaccine, so only senior citizens, which I was still years away from being, were getting shots. I remember standing in a line in a hallway at my clinic, the only non–senior citizen waiting to get a jab. When it was my turn, I stepped into a little room where a nurse was administering the shots. She looked at me and said, "What's your story?" I told her. She said, "That's a good story," and gave me a shot.

IN 1975, REBELS FROM Zaire had kidnapped four researchers from Gombe. When we arrived there, park staff assured us that we had security. Walking along the lakeshore trail that first evening, we did meet the Gombe security guard. He had a bow and three arrows. In travel moments like this your mindset is key to coping with uneasy circumstances. The affirming thought to remember is, "right now, we are fine." Italian novelist and poet Cesare Pavese wrote, "Travel forces you to trust strangers and to lose sight of all that familiar comfort of home and friends."

Upon arrival at Gombe, we had to quarantine outside the forest for five days to protect the chimpanzees. After that time, a nurse examined us, taking our temperature, listening to our heart and lungs, and reviewing our medical history. Since we had time before we were allowed to track the chimpanzees, we took a hike from the lakeshore to the top of the park. It takes half a day to hike up through forest to the open grassland ridge that forms the eastern boundary of the park. Like any uphill hike off any established trail through a forest, it was invigorating, and we stopped along the way to hydrate. Near the top, the forest gave way to open grassland, which encouraged our final push to the summit. A reward awaited us. From the top of the park, we had a spectacular view of the lake, with the Democratic Republic of the Congo on the other side. And with a cool breeze coming off the lake, the moment was idyllic. Everyone sat silently on the hilltop without conversation. Our entire group organically shared a moment of mindfulness—observe the present as it is.

TRAINED TANZANIANS AS STAFF of the Gombe Stream Research Centre go out daily and follow chimpanzees and record observations. Once a chimpanzee builds its nest for the night, the staff can head home knowing they can go back to that nest the next morning to follow a specific chimp. The study of the Gombe chimpanzees is the longest running and uninterrupted field study of animals in the wild. Research at Gombe has resulted in more than thirty-five PhD theses and more than thirty books.

When that research staff learned that I had come from Minnesota, they asked me to carry hand-recorded field notes back to the "Jane Goodall's Institute for Primate Studies" at the University of Minnesota. They gave me forty pounds of notes, which I packed in the duffle that I planned to carry on my flight out of Nairobi to Amsterdam to Minneapolis. Upon check-in at the Nairobi airport, I learned that my carry-on was over the weight limit. I had to transfer a large stack of field notes from my duffle to my checked luggage. I was afraid the bag might be lost along the way. If that happened, I would be forever known as the guy who interrupted the longest uninterrupted study of animals in the wild. Fortunately, the field notes arrived back to Minnesota safely.

WE RECEIVED FUNDING TO do a pilot shoot in Gombe from the Informal Science Education Directorate of the US National Science Foundation. There was a question of whether one could do a documentary on the ongoing research at Gombe and successfully film wild chimpanzees with a large and noisy IMAX camera. The camera was big. It sounded a bit like a power lawn mower running. We sent in a small crew with a single camera, one tripod, and a few rolls of film hoping they could capture footage that would demonstrate this was a story that had to be told in IMAX.

Wildlife and weather do not take film direction well. An element of good fortune is required to make a film like this. One day, the crew got a shot of a chimpanzee termite fishing. The sun came out from behind a cloud in the middle of the shot at a perfect time to illuminate the action with natural daylight. Thanks to this moment, we got the footage we needed to garner support for sending in a full film crew to Gombe to produce a forty-minute documentary for IMAX theaters around the world.

While the film was in production, the National Science Foundation supported an Educator Institute in conjunction with the film. Twenty teams of two—a museum educator paired with a classroom teacher—came from across North America to spend a week in Saint Paul learning about the work that had been done in Gombe and taking advantage of the access to the field notes and the researchers at the University of Minnesota. These educators designed an array of educational enhancement materials and activities so that viewers, especially students, would be able to see the film at their local museum and then explore further. Our intent was always to magnify the educational mission of a film by leveraging the resources of a worldwide museum community.

Jane Goodall's Wild Chimpanzees premiered in the IMAX Theatre at Science North in Sudbury. The next day, we hosted a press screening in Toronto. One reviewer wrote, "It opens up a little corner of the world that even casual observers had long ago heard about, but have rarely seen." When the film played in San Diego at the Fleet Science Center, home to the first IMAX Dome Theater in the world, the *Union Tribune* wrote, "There's enough science to make it count as educational, and enough beauty to make it unforgettable." And a review in *The Big Movie Zone* wrote, "The film gets close to the chimps the same way Goodall did, with a serious-minded patience, respect, and affection."

Developing patience, respect, and embracing uncertainty grows your mindset. Growing your mindset makes you better not only at traveling to distant places but also in reaching positive outcomes in everyday life.

VISITOR'S ENTRY PERMIT
Immigration Control Act, 1993
(Sections 9 and 29/Regulation 2)

Granted in terms of Act 7 of 1993 for the purpose of holiday/tourism/business for a period not exceeding 90 calender days as from the date of entry. Employment in any form is prohibited.

IMMIGRATION OFFICER
ESPINOZA
(La Paz, B...)
VT-16

Republic of Namibia — Immigration
ENTRY STAMP
22 MAR 1995
1A — J.G. STRIJDOM AIRPORT

IMMIGRATION SERVICE
4 DEC 1985
DEPARTED (2100)
HONG KONG

Visitor Permitted to re... until 30 DEC 1985

FOR VISIT / VIR BESOEK
PURPOSE OF VISIT MAY NOT BE CHANGED / DOEL VAN BESOEK MAG NIE VERANDER WORD NIE

DIRECCION GENERAL DE MIGRACION
SALIDA
14.3.94
VALENCIA

25 MAR 1988
COSTA RICA

03

WHAT TO SEEK

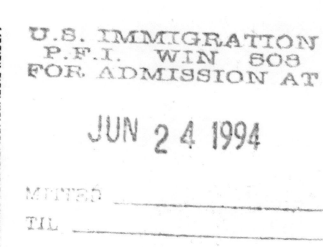

Chapter 11

SEEK CULTURE

Valencia

VALENCIA IS A COASTAL river town, where the Turia River flows into the Mediterranean Sea. In 1957, the river flooded and caused tremendous damage to the city. More than eighty people perished. The river was drained and diverted to run around the city. The old river valley through the city is now a parkway, called the Garden of Turia, with bikeways and walkways along with gardens, playgrounds, and football pitches. Beautiful cultural centers have been built in the parkway. Santiago Calatrava, the world-famous structural engineer and architect who was born in Valencia, designed the City of Arts in the old Turia riverway. Several books have a list of places you must visit, or events you must attend, before you die. At the top of any list should be the Falles Festival in Valencia, Spain.

The annual celebration culminates on March 19, the feast day of St. Joseph, the patron saint of carpenters. Falles, from the Latin word *fax* (meaning torch), refers to the festival as well as its monuments. Every year, each neighborhood works to design and build a four-to-five-story-high *falle*. Each one is an original, unique, and beautifully crafted sculpture made of a wood framework covered in papier-mâché and splendidly painted. The creations lampoon people, often worldwide politicians and movie stars, in alluring and offensive poses. Residents build more than five hundred of these satirical sculptures in the town squares. On the last night of the festival, all the *falles* are set on fire and burned down.

During the five-day Falles Festival, brass bands march down the streets and people light strings of fireworks along the boulevards, beginning early in the morning and continuing all day. It is a weeklong street party with continuous parades and people, including children throwing fireworks and noisemakers. In the evening, large pans of paella, a dish of rice, chicken, rabbit, or seafood, simmer over outdoor bonfires.

As a city on the east coast of Spain with miles of Mediterranean coastline, Valencia offers plenty of seafood. A great meal in Valencia starts with an appetizer of clóchinas, or small Mediterranean mussels. Drive an hour south of Valencia to Ganda, where you'll find *fideuà*, a dish of thin buckwheat noodles with seafood such as shrimp and squid. Ganda holds an annual *fideuà* cooking contest each year. Valencia also offers a local favorite, *all i pebre,* a hot stew with potatoes and eel. Treats such as *bunyols,* a sweet fritter with a bit of pumpkin in the dough, along with *fartons,* a sweet bread glazed with sugar, are plentiful on the streets of Valencia, especially during *Las Fallas.*

At 2:00 p.m. every day during Falles, all the shops close and everyone heads to the city center and the main square. On the steps of city hall, the *Fallera Major,* Queen of the Falles, declares that "the pyrotechnicians may commence the *Mascletà.*" A cacophony of aerial gunpowder explosions, like thousands of cannons going off at an ever-increasing rate, fill the city center with louder and louder blasts and billowing clouds of smoke. With the last blast, the crowd applauds and whistles for the pyrotechnicians, who come across the streets bordering the city center to shake hands with the joyous and appreciative audience.

I had the pleasure of visiting the Falles Festival twice. When I visited as a board member of an international IMAX theater consortium, our hosts from L'Hemisfèric, Valencia's IMAX

Dome theater, part of the City of Arts and Sciences, treated us to great seats for the *Mascletà* on the balcony of city hall. The sights and sounds were extraordinary.

THE PEOPLE OF VALENCIA keep later hours than those of us from the United States, so we were always one of the first groups to populate the night spots. One evening, we were treated to glasses of *agua de Valencia*, a splash of gin and vodka with cava or champagne in a glass with ice cubes and juice from sweet Valencia oranges.

In the 1978 book *Valencia, Noche*, you can find the origin story of *agua de Valencia*. Basque visitors drinking cava one night in Valencia called it *agua de Bilbao*, or the water of Bilbao. The bartender created a variation for them, offering it as *agua de Valencia*.

When my colleagues and I were working on our fourth glass of *aqua de Valencia*, one of our hosts said we should plan on stopping after two. She hadn't noticed that we had passed that number an hour or so earlier.

We returned to the hotel that evening under a light rain. One of our colleagues came to breakfast the next morning and told us she had tried to dry out the leather jacket she was wearing the night before over a lamp shade with the light turned on. Between the jet lag and the *aqua de Valencia*, she quickly fell asleep. She awoke to the smell of her jacket smoldering atop the light. We envisioned being lost in a great hotel fire during the Falles Festival. For the rest of our trip, we limited ourselves each evening to no more than two *agua de Valencias*.

IN THE EVENING HOURS during the Falles Festival, the pyrotechnicians go to work with a traditional fireworks display from the old river valley. Balconies overlooking the valley are covered with screening to protect them from the firework casings that rain down from the sky.

Many residents wear historical, often medieval, outfits from Catalonian history, especially for the offering of flowers that takes place March 17 and 18 in the Plaza de la Virgin. During this decoration of a multistory statue of Our Lady of the Forsaken, the patron saint of Valencia, groups parade to the site carrying bouquets of flowers. They throw the flowers to workers clinging to the wooden frame that supports the image of St. Joseph's spouse, Mary. Workers place the flowers within the frame to create a living floral gown of the Virgin Mary.

One origin story of the Falles, which dates to the eighteenth century, tells that during the winter months, carpenters burned shavings and scraps of wood in their workshops for evening illumination and warmth. With the coming of spring and the increase in daylight and warmer nights, the carpenters saved the scraps and then burned their piles on the feast day of their patron saint, St. Joseph. Given that the feast day coincides with the vernal equinox, the festival's origins may also have a foundation from pagan times.

One of the most revered customs of the Falles Festival is the role of a *fallera*, a young woman elected to represent the falle figure from her neighborhood. One of the strongest images I took away from the festival was of these women in traditional costumes on the culmination of the festival, posing for photos in front of their burned and fallen *falle*. Many of the *fallera* weep at this finale, recognizing the privilege of the role, which is an honor that will likely happen only once in their lifetime.

The day after the Falles Festival, fireworks are outlawed in Valencia until next year.

Chapter 12

SEEK AUTHENTICITY

STOCKHOLM & AMSTERDAM

SWEDEN SHARES A LONG border with the Baltic Sea, and in Swedish maritime history the most famous ship is the *Vasa*. The story of the Swedish warship *Vasa* can be told several different ways—as a TV show, a lecture, a book, or even an IMAX film. However, the story as it is told in Stockholm is the most powerful because the story is bound by authenticity.

In 1625, the Swedish Navy lost ten ships during the Thirty Years' War, and the commander of the Hapsburg Empire was at the Baltic. This was a serious threat to Sweden. King Gustavus Adolphus needed to expand his naval fleet, so he commissioned the construction of the warship *Vasa*.

The completed ship was 220 feet long. It flew ten sails and carried sixty-four cannons. It was ornamented with seven hundred sculptures and carvings, including a ten-foot-long carved figurehead at the bow of the boat of a roaring lion with a protruding tongue leading a procession of twenty Roman emperors. Six carved knights in armor flanked the admiral's cabin windows. A depiction at the top of the stern conveyed the king as a young boy with long flowing hair, being crowned by two griffins—legendary creatures with the body, back legs, and tail of a lion and the head and wings of an eagle. Dominating the stern carvings were two lions holding the shields found in the national coat of arms. Below it, angels held sheaves of grain, symbols of the royal family.

On the afternoon of Sunday, August 10, 1628, the captain of the newly built *Vasa* gave the order to cast off. Vespers were over and churches were emptying. Many of Stockholm's ten thousand people came out to enjoy the summer afternoon and witness the *Vasa*'s departure.

With only four sails hoisted, the ship moved slowly. A strong gust from the hilltops made her heel, but then she straightened up. As the ship sailed out of the protection of its port, the wind had freer play. A gust caused the *Vasa* to heel once more. This time, water rushed in the gun ports until the *Vasa*'s railing was in the water. Her destiny had come. The maiden voyage lasted less than two hours. The *Vasa* sank to the bottom of Stockholm harbor, before it could reach the Baltic Sea, with flags flying, sails full, and all on board.

No one knows how many people were on the ship. The crew should have consisted of 130 seamen, but families were also allowed on the first leg of a maiden voyage. No list has ever been found of those who were saved and those who drowned.

The Swedes had a long record of marine architecture, carrying an inheritance from the Vikings. But during the construction of the *Vasa*, King Gustavus Adolphus requested design changes. The king had learned that the Danes were building a ship with two gun decks, so he ordered two for the *Vasa*. This would add height and weight above the waterline, and no one in Sweden had ever built a ship with two gun decks. The primary designer was not working from plans, and he didn't have detailed specifications. Then he died a year before the ship was completed.

The *Vasa* had been poorly engineered. The ship was too narrow, the superstructure was too high, and its bronze cannons made it too top heavy. It never had a sailing chance.

SEEK AUTHENTICITY

The *Vasa* sat on the seabed for more than 330 years. No glorious deeds, no war stories, no battles against stormy seas. She never made any contribution in defense of Sweden. But the *Vasa* is still in a class of her own: she is the world's oldest identified completely restored ship.

The *Vasa* sank in a perfect setting to preserve it for hundreds of years. It sank upright and intact, in enough depth (about one hundred feet) to protect it from ultraviolet light. The wreck was in a sheltered harbor that protected it from storms. The harbor's cold water minimized deterioration. The oxygen-poor, brackish water—a mix of fresh water, salt water, and sulfates from sewage running into the harbor—protected it from microbial decay and worms that digest the wrecks of wooden ships.

In 1957, work began to salvage the *Vasa*. It was a herculean effort, involving more than 1,300 dives to dig channels under the sunken ship. Divers strung a dozen six-inch cables through these channels. A series of eighteen lifts and short hauls of the boat moved it incrementally back to shore.

April 24, 1961, was resurrection day: the oak structure of the seventeenth-century ship made its first appearance out of the water. Over the hours, the *Vasa* slowly emerged. It was soon possible to make out the contour of the deck. On the foredeck, a pair of carved wooden knightheads appeared. Ropes to maneuver the foremast sails still ran through the sheave holes in the knightheads. At 2:00 p.m. that afternoon, a worker stepped onto the deck of the *Vasa*, the first person to do so in more than 330 years.

In 1988, the *Vasa* made her final voyage through the open end of the Vasa Museum, then under construction. It is the most visited museum in Scandinavia. It is one of the world's most popular and highly regarded museums, even though it is built around a single object.

A visit to the museum is dramatic not only because of its

engrossing historical story, but because we have the ship. If we were to learn this story any other way, it would be an interesting story. But it would be nowhere near as captivating and enlightening as the experience delivered not with a recreation or a model, but by the authentic artifact.

I HAVE SOUGHT OUT the power of authenticity in my travels, including during a visit to Amsterdam. Having read Anne Frank's diary, I wanted to visit the house where she, her family, and four others, all Jews, went into hiding from the Nazis.

In 1940, Anne Frank's father moved the spice company he worked for to a house in central Amsterdam. The ground floor held the spice mills and warehouse. The second floor held offices. A steep set of narrow stairs led to a rear annex where Anne, her father, mother, sister, and four others hid during the Nazi occupation. A moveable bookcase was positioned in front of the stairway that led to their hiding place, a secret annex of 450 square feet.

Anne Frank had received a blank diary for her thirteenth birthday on June 12, 1942. On July 6, the family went into hiding. Anne kept writing in her diary as they remained hidden for two years and one month. They were then captured by the Nazis and deported to their deaths in concentration camps. Of the group, only Anne's father survived the camps. He later retrieved Anne's diary, which has now been published in more than seventy languages.

Anne decorated her room in their hiding place with pictures cut from magazines. On July 11, 1942, she wrote, "Thanks to Father, who brought my whole collection of picture postcards and movie stars here beforehand, I have been able to treat the walls with a pot of glue and a brush and so turn the entire room into one big picture."

SEEK AUTHENTICITY

When I made my pilgrimage to the house where Anne Frank and her family hid, the bookcase was pushed aside. I, along with other visitors, ascended the staircase to the Frank family hiding place. The original wallpaper and authentic pictures were still on the wall of her room.

The Vasa Museum and the Anne Frank House are two of the sites I have visited around the world that affected me because of their authenticity. I have been blessed to travel to many similar sites. Others include the Tenement Museum on the lower east side of Manhattan, a restored building that opened in 1869 with twenty-two apartments and a basement saloon. For more than sixty years, it housed immigrants, migrants, and refugees to the United States. Then there is the Gold Museum in Bogotá, which exhibits pre-Columbian artifacts that showcase the incredible artistry and cultures before the arrival of the Spanish in the Americas. The US Holocaust Memorial Museum in Washington, D.C., includes a powerful display of four thousand pairs of shoes—the actual shoes worn by arrivals to a Nazi death camp. And at the Rosa Parks Museum in Montgomery, Alabama, you'll find a 1955 city bus like the one on which Rosa Parks was arrested after breaking a segregation law and refusing to give up her seat to a white passenger.

I can't fathom taking a holiday to an amusement park when I could journey to Amsterdam, Bogotá, Washington, D.C., Montgomery, or Stockholm. Seek out the places, the museums, and the cultural centers that invite you to witness the authentic pieces of our human experience.

Chapter 13

SEEK THE LOCALS' FAVORITES

TOKYO

IN OUR FAMILY, WHEN children reach the age of seven or eight, we take them on their first airplane trip. I remember well the glee of their smiles and wide eyes at that first experience of taking off. Flight is a miracle of humankind, and one is warmly reminded of that when they take a young person on their first plane ride. As filmmaker Brian Terwilliger scripted in his splendid documentary film *Living in the Age of Airplanes*, "No virtual technology can ever do what the airplane does."

In giving one of my nephews the gift of travel, I began taking him on trips each March during his school spring break, beginning when he was eight years old. Traveling with him I sought out the best guides to immerse ourselves better, rather than skip across the surface of the places we visited. When I took my nephew to San Francisco we signed up for a morning walking tour and lunch with Linda Lee, a woman who grew up in Chinatown. There was no better way to explore the neighborhood than with someone who had lived there and could take us into places through the backdoor, which casual tourists would never discover.

WHAT TO SEEK

THE FIRST SPRING BREAK trip with my eight-year-old nephew was to Chicago, my hometown, a terrific place to explore with children. The next year, we went to St. Louis. The highlights of our trip included a visit to the St. Louis Science Center and the City Museum, which is better described as a playground on steroids. Then, when my nephew was ten, I figured he was old enough to answer the question: "Where would you like to go?" He said, "New York . . . or Tokyo." So, when he was ten, we went to New York, and when he was twelve, we boarded a Delta flight from Minneapolis to Tokyo.

NO MATTER HOW YOU count the population of a city—as the metropolitan area, the urban area, or the commuter area—the most populated city on the planet is Tokyo. The metropolitan population approaches forty million people. It may be the most orderly city on Earth. I watched someone in the airport pick up a dropped scarf, fold it, and lay it back down. If you drop something in Tokyo, retrace your steps. Someone probably has found it and left it neatly in place so you can return to find it. If you want to know which subway to take, stand in front of a wall map in the station. Someone will come and offer to help you. If you are like me, an English speaker knowing little Japanese, they will speak English with you. They won't just point you in the direction you should go, they will walk you to where you need to be to catch the right train.

Japan transposes names. What I think of as my first name—Mike—the Japanese treat as my last name. Upon checking into the hotel, the desk clerk said, "Welcome, Mr. Me-Kay."

The hotel my nephew and I stayed at had cabs out front all day and night. I told my nephew to expect jet lag, and depending on when we might be awake, we may head out to try and get a spot to observe firsthand a "must-see" event: the daily tuna auction at the Tsukiji Fish Market. The largest wholesale seafood and fish market in the world, it replaced a previous market that had been destroyed in the Great Kanto earthquake of 1923. Work began at the market at 3:00 a.m. for thousands of workers who process and sell four hundred kinds of seafood, such as sea urchin, scallops, abalone, squid, eel, and giant oysters. At its height, the Tsukiji Market moved five million pounds of seafood daily. It admitted only 150 visitors early each morning to watch the tuna auction on a first-come, first-served basis.

Our second morning in Tokyo, we were awake at 3:30 a.m. We dressed, got in a cab, and headed to the tuna auction. We were numbers 141 and 142 in line and it wasn't even 5:00 a.m. The 150 of us fortunate enough to watch the auction had to wait outside in the dark of a cool morning in Tokyo. We were from all over the world.

After an hour, staff led us into a building and gave us colored vests to wear while we continued to wait. It was 6:30 a.m. when we finally were ushered in a single file line to the market floor to hear the ringing of the handbell by the shouting auctioneer standing on a box. Being unfamiliar with the language added to the drama of the event for us, as well as the excitement about what we were seeing in a jet-lagged state less than forty-eight hours after we arrived in Japan.

Somewhat surprisingly, the Pacific bluefin tuna, each more than 250 pounds, arrived at the market frozen with their heads and tails cut off. Potential buyers walked along rows of tuna, poking at the red meat of the tail section to determine the quality of the meat.

After operating for more than eighty years, the Tsukiji tuna auction was relocated to Tokyo's new Toyosu Fish Market. No longer do you get to wait in line outside in the dark with people from around the world for an opportunity to see the auction. Nor do you get to stand on the floor of the market. Now you pre-register online to get a ticket and you watch from a visitor gallery above the floor. It means you might miss the opportunity my nephew remembers well of almost being run over by a Japanese forklift driver during the early morning activity in the world's largest fish market.

After the tuna auction, we decided we should next visit what all visitors to Tokyo should set as a destination: Mount Fuji. What we remember most, however, was not the misty peak but the train trip at the end of our day. We took a bus tour to Mount Fuji, with additional stops afterward. At the end of the day, we were dropped at a station to catch a train back to Tokyo. We stood on a train platform with the track below. The platform and track for trains going in the opposite direction were across the way. Between the two tracks was a third track. As we stood waiting for our train, we heard what sounded like a jet landing and watched a bullet train fly by on the middle track without slowing down. Our mouths hung open, being only a stone's throw away from a train passing at almost two hundred miles an hour. The Shinkansen, Japan's high speed bullet train rail line, has never had a fatal accident in more than fifty years. The bullet train is so punctual that the train company issued an apology in 2017, when a train departed twenty seconds ahead of schedule.

In advance of the Tokyo trip, I followed the reports from Japan on the cherry blossoms. Like the fall colors in North America, the blooming of the cherry blossoms in Japan prompts close attention with hopes one might be in the right place at the right time to catch the peak bloom. The Saturday my nephew and I were scheduled to fly from Minneapolis to Tokyo, we checked a Japanese website that reports on the cherry blossom bloom across the country. The site said this was the week to be in Tokyo.

With its eight hundred cherry trees, Tokyo's thirteen-acre Ueno Park was our primary destination to see cherry blossoms.

SEEK THE LOCALS' FAVORITES

We were lucky to be there on a sunny day when the blossoms were in full beautiful bloom. At night, lanterns lit the park. People gathered for food, drink, songs, companionship, and the beauty of *sakura*, cherry blossoms. We felt privileged to be part of the crowd strolling amidst the extraordinary abundance of blossoms filling the trees.

Ueno Park at the peak of the cherry blossoms was magical. Many people came early to stake out a space by taping down blue tarps so they had room to gather later, usually with coworkers. There was a distinct contrast between the beauty of the cherry trees in bloom above us and the bright blue polypropylene tarps secured with gray industrial tape on the ground.

The practice of gathering under the cherry trees was popularized during the Heian period in Japan (the years 794–1185). His Majesty Emperor Saga adopted the custom and organized parties where he drank sake and celebrated the flowering of sakura trees in the Imperial Court of Kyoto. Today, companies often send a younger recruit to tape down the blue tarp to reserve the spot until coworkers arrive. A great deal of beer and sake is consumed.

WHILE I HAD VISITED Japan many times for my work, my trip with my nephew was my first as a tourist. One of the best business relationships I had was with Goto, an optical company that made planetarium projectors and telescopes for educational institutions around the world. They also made a fish-eye projection system for films on planetarium domes. We sold them rights to own and distribute films in Asia. We would use their cash to support financing the production, which we then distributed elsewhere in the world. In a business relationship with such an established and esteemed Japanese company, gift-giving was protocol. It started with a small exchange of items and over time graduated upward from there. We reached a point where we commissioned a gift that would be hand-crafted from wood.

Japanese culture is saturated with reverence for wood. Most of the trees in Japan are in conservation areas. Most structures in Japan are made with wood: homes, shrines, temples, and castles. The ladle and whisk used in a tea ceremony are made from bamboo. Rice mixing tubs, the bath stools upon which one sits to bathe before entering a hot spring, the Torii gates that mark the entrance to a shrine, the Bento box, and chopsticks—all are made from wood. The Buddha attained enlightenment meditating under a tree.

The CEO of our partner company always had his golf clubs in his car. We had commissioned a wooden golf putter with his signature engraved in the face, along with a cedar box to hold it. It was designed and constructed following the Japanese legacy of using interlocking joints instead of metal screws. Our gift cost thousands of dollars, and our host was grateful when presented with it upon our arrival to his office in Tokyo. He stepped to his desk and picked up the business card for the head of a company with whom he had a long-standing relationship. Our host handed us the card and said, "Please make another one of these putters for this gentleman."

A woman by the name of Natsuko worked for the company. She was assigned to be my host on a couple of my business trips. She lost her job during the "Lost Decades," a period of economic stagnation in Japan. She next began working as a tour guide and photographer. As having the right guide can make a day of travel unlike any other, I hired her without hesitation for the first day my nephew and I were in Tokyo. She met us at our hotel and our greeting began with traditional gift giving. She had been a fan of the *Ally McBeal* TV series, which starred Calista Flockhart as a young attorney, so I gifted her three full seasons of the program on DVD.

SEEK THE LOCALS' FAVORITES

The first place she took us on a beautiful spring day was Meiji Shrine, built between 1915 and 1926 and rebuilt after being destroyed in World War II. It is dedicated to Emperor Meiji and Empress Shōken. The shrine is amid a 175-acre forest that includes the wishing tree, where visitors write and hang their wishes. The Emperor Meiji, who is also called Meiji the Good, led Japan through a rapid period of economic, social, and political modernization from an isolated feudal country. In the first days of a new year, the shrine welcomes more than three million visitors for the first prayers of the year.

The second stop on our tour was to Sensō-ji Temple, the oldest temple in Tokyo. The pathway to the temple is through the Thunder Gate, which stands forty feet tall with a massive red paper lantern hanging from its center. The original gate was built in the year 941. It has burned down on multiple occasions, but is always rebuilt.

The street from the Thunder Gate to the temple runs three hundred yards, and it is lined with scores of shops. The shops have operated since the seventeenth century, run by generations of the same families who cater to pilgrims coming to the shrine. You can buy kimonos, chopsticks, samurai swords, Buddhist scrolls, Godzilla toys, and maneki-neko, the "beckoning cats." They are statuettes, usually ceramic, of a seated cat with one paw raised. A cat with its left paw raised brings customers to a business. A right paw raised brings good fortune and wealth.

Natsuko had promised we would go to her favorite lunch place. Since it was late in the afternoon, and the restaurant was a few train stops away, she suggested that we might then lunch in the neighborhood we were in. I told her no thank you—we had traveled all the way to Tokyo, and our traveling bodies weren't in sync with any mealtimes. We had to take the time to go to her favorite place. We rode the train and got off in an indistinct neighborhood, walked down indistinct streets, and came to a small, indistinct restaurant doorway. The greeting we received, even though in a language I did not understand, made it obvious that she was a regular there.

If you had given me the address for this restaurant, I am sure I could never have found it, given the little doorway and the lack of any distinction. We sat upstairs with the kitchen adjoining, and had a simple, but splendid Japanese meal of soba noodles and rice. Natusko instructed my nephew on the proper etiquette of using chopsticks, including never sticking them standing straight up in the rice. It is bad luck, as it is only done in a funeral ritual.

Natsuko had emailed diligently prior to our trip to Japan to ask where we wanted to go and what we wanted to see. I wrote her to tell her the only thing on my nephew's list was that he wanted to buy original Japanese Yu-Gi-Oh trading cards. The trading card game launched in Japan in 1999 and in 2002 in North America. My nephew had a large collection of the cards, which he had purchased at Target stores in Minnesota. The game had sold more than thirty-five billion cards worldwide. Thanks to hiring Natsuko as our guide, we fulfilled my nephew's wish at one of the Kiddy Land stores in Tokyo. He became the first kid in his school to show up with Yu-Gi-Oh trading cards—all in Japanese.

My nephew's appetite for a Japanese card game, hiring a local to act as a guide, and getting up at 3:30 a.m. all encouraged me in my future travels to immerse myself deeper into each place, each culture, each person.

Chapter 14

DON'T FEAR A WRONG TURN

Montgomery & Iceland

PRIOR TO THE COVID-19 pandemic, my spouse and I had made plans to go to the 2020 summer Olympics in Tokyo. I had been to Japan several times and was eager to take her, as she had never been. And in all our travels over the years, neither one of us had ever been to an Olympics.

We worked with a broker to secure hotel accommodations, transportation, and, most importantly, tickets to our preferred events. We planned to see the women's basketball championship game, as well as track-and-field events in the newly built 68,000-seat National Stadium in Tokyo.

We paid for refundable airline tickets and purchased insurance in case there was an interruption to our Olympic travel plans. Alas, the pandemic forced the postponement of the summer Olympics until 2021. We were content to wait another year. Then, four months prior to the rescheduled games, the Japanese decided to limit spectators, prohibiting travelers from outside of Japan. We had protected ourselves for an extraordinary and unpredictable scenario. All the money we had already paid for the trip was returned to us. We stayed home and watched the competitions streamed, like the rest of the world.

WHAT TO SEEK

WHEN THE NEWS HIT about the Olympics going forward without fans in the stands, I was disappointed for the lost opportunity, and then started researching where and when we might leave the United States again. I listened to podcasts and pored over news articles about travel options and COVID safety measures being implemented around the world. Due to Canada's travel restrictions, we couldn't even drive the 135 miles from our cabin on Lake Superior's north shore to cross the international border. Canada wouldn't let us in.

I went to the US Centers for Disease Control (CDC) website to read the risk assessment for countries worldwide. They divided the world into color-coded levels of risk—from low risk (Level 1) to very high risk (Level 4). At the start of summer 2021, fifteen months after the World Health Organization had declared the pandemic, countries to which I had previously enjoyed traveling to (or was interested in exploring for a first time) still carried a very high CDC risk label: Sweden, Costa Rica, Namibia, Trinidad, Madagascar, and Estonia. Canada was rated Level 3: high risk.

The place that finally rose to the top of my list was one I had never visited, a place to which I could get a direct flight, and a place with a CDC Level 1 risk: Iceland. I began talking to those who had been there. I went to the library and borrowed a copy of Rick Steves's *Guide to Iceland*. I made numerous visits to the Trip Advisor app on my phone to read travelers' stories from Iceland.

Even with all my research and planning, an unexpected turn meant that my first distant trip since the COVID pandemic was declared wasn't to Iceland. It turned out to be to a place that wasn't even on my list.

DON'T FEAR A WRONG TURN

MY EIGHTEEN-YEAR-OLD NIECE HAD been accepted to attend Alabama State University (ASU) in Montgomery, Alabama. Though it was at the top of her list, she had not had a chance to visit the campus during the pandemic. Two months before her freshman year was set to begin, with both of us fully vaccinated, we flew to Atlanta and drove on to Montgomery. It was the first time I had been on an airplane in 487 days.

As first-time travelers to Montgomery, my niece and I had one objective: to take a scheduled ninety-minute tour of the ASU campus with two current students. We drove onto the campus the night before the tour to begin to get acquainted with the place. What we discovered, both on the campus and around Montgomery, were a lot of buildings with historical markers in front of them. Montgomery has a lot of history, especially with respect to the civil rights movement of the 1950s and 1960s.

The best travel experiences are so often the unplanned ones. As Anthony Bourdain said, "I'm a big believer in winging it. Letting the happy accident happen is what a lot of vacation itineraries miss."

On the day of our campus tour, I made a wrong turn and had us going in the opposite direction of where I intended. Instead of driving down South Jackson Street to the campus of Alabama State University, I drove *up* the street. We had plenty of time, so we purposely continued in the wrong direction, letting the happy accident happen. We spotted a house on South Jackson Street that bore a historical marker. We pulled over. It was the Dexter Parsonage House. Built in 1912, it was the house for the pastor of the Dexter Baptist Church. In 1954, a new pastor came to live here at the age of twenty-five. His name was Martin Luther King Jr.

WHAT TO SEEK

ON THURSDAY EVENING, DECEMBER 1, 1955, Rosa Parks boarded the Cleveland Avenue bus, headed home from her job as a seamstress in a department store in downtown Montgomery. She was seated just ahead of the "colored section." When the white seats at the front of the bus filled, the bus driver asked Parks and three other Black riders to move to the back to make room for white riders. Rosa Parks refused.

The bus driver pulled over and stepped off the bus to use a pay phone to report the incident. The police came and arrested Parks. E.D. Nixon, a Black community leader, bailed her out of jail. She was scheduled to appear in court the following Monday.

On the tour of the campus, my niece and I found ourselves in front of Alabama State University's Council Hall. It was here on the evening that Rosa Parks was arrested that Jo Ann Robinson, an English professor at Alabama State and the president of the Women's Political Council, typed up a statement so that it appeared three times on a single sheet of paper. In part, it said, "If we do not do something to stop these arrests, they will continue . . . this woman's case will come up on Monday . . . stay off the buses Monday in protest of the arrest and trial."

Robinson and two students stayed up all night and mimeographed more than ten thousand copies of the page, cutting each into three for distribution throughout the Black community of Montgomery. Black ministers announced the boycott in church. They formed an association and chose Martin Luther King Jr. as its head. They called for the boycott to continue beyond a single day, and the Montgomery bus strike began.

A group of Black women challenged a city ordinance and State of Alabama statute and won in US District Court, overturning the busing segregation laws. The city appealed to the US Supreme Court, which upheld the lower court's ruling and delivered the order on December 20, 1956. The next day the city buses were integrated and the Montgomery bus strike ended after 381 days.

WITH THE MONTGOMERY TRIP under our belts, I turned my focus to the originally planned trip to Iceland. In September 2021, my spouse and I made our first sojourn out of the United States in 555 days. It was a direct flight from Minneapolis to Reykjavík. We rented a vehicle and spent a week driving the Golden Circle in southern Iceland—a 150-mile loop that connects Reykjavík and parts of the country's most beautiful scenery. We ate cured salmon, arctic char, Atlantic wolffish, and North Atlantic plaice. We hiked six hours to overlook the crater of the volcano Fagradalsfjall, which had become active six months before our visit.

When my spouse and I joined thousands of others traveling to Iceland's active volcano in 2021, we didn't go blindly. We knew the only way to eliminate the risk of getting hurt or even losing our lives was to not be there. We hired an Icelandic guide, who had been escorting groups there for months before we arrived. He carried a gas monitor and led us up to higher elevations when the air was risky closer to the lava field. Volcanic gas can contain sulfur dioxide, carbon dioxide, and hydrogen sulfide. Our guide carried gas masks. Fortunately, we didn't need them that day.

Even visiting a volcano with licensed, experienced guides who work under the approval of a government agency does not eliminate the risk. White Island, thirty miles off the coast of the North Island of New Zealand, was once a popular destination for people seeking to climb a volcano. On December 9, 2019, the volcano erupted. Twenty-five were injured, many with severe burns, and twenty-two were killed.

WHAT TO SEEK

ICELAND IS THE NEWEST island on Earth. Its landscapes date back to less than twenty million years ago, when magma rose from beneath the Earth's mantle along the mid-Atlantic ridge as the North American and Eurasian tectonic plates slid away from each other. The process continues today. Iceland has seen hundreds of volcanic eruptions since the Norse arrived there sometime in the ninth century.

Ingólfur Arnarson is credited with establishing the first permanent settlement in Iceland. In 874, he followed a Viking ritual, tossing high-seat pillars into the sea as he approached land. The pillars, symbols of the authority of a chieftain during Viking times, were wooden poles placed on each side of a tall seat where the head of the community sat. The settler's home would be established where the gods brought the pillars. Arnarson called the place where his pillars went ashore Reykjavík. In the early tenth century, Icelanders held a district assembly near Reykjavík. This evolved into an annual event, a National Assembly held for more than eight hundred years at a site that is today Thingvellir National Park. This assembly went on to become the world's first parliamentary government.

In Thingvellir the great underwater mid-Atlantic ridge exposes itself above sea level. There we hiked between two great plates of the earth that continue to split apart. As we overnighted near the park, we found ourselves on several mornings and evenings driving through it. Every time we did, the beauty of the landscape overwhelmed us, whether the sky was full sunshine, floating clouds, or a gray sky with misty rain. Ravines opened by tectonic movement are filled with glacier meltwater and the undulating lava rock terrain is mottled with moss. The interaction of light and landscape created vistas that made us feel we were elsewhere in space and time. It was easy to understand why the park was used as the setting for the "Gates of the Moon" in the HBO series *Game of Thrones*.

DON'T FEAR A WRONG TURN

A long period of peace in Iceland came to an end beginning in the early thirteenth century, when power struggles fueled the creation of chieftain armies that raided each other across the country. In 1281, the king of Norway introduced a new code of law, along with high taxes. The volcano Hekla erupted three times, covering a large part of the island in ash, and a mini-ice age wiped out crops and livestock. Then the Black Death came to Iceland, killing half of its population.

In the 1600s, pirates arrived in Iceland, and hundreds of Icelanders were captured and sold as slaves in Algiers. A smallpox epidemic killed tens of thousands of people in the early 1700s. The Katla volcano erupted in 1660, Hekla in 1693, Katla again in 1721 and 1755, and Hekla again in 1766.

The 1783–84 eruption of the volcano Laki lasted eight months, covering the island in ash and a sulfuric acid fog that killed crops and livestock and led to the death of more than 20 percent of the population, mostly from starvation. Denmark considered relocating the remaining Icelandic population to their country. In 1800, it was about 45,000 people.

In the twentieth century, Iceland transformed from a poor country into one of the most developed. Early in the century its rowboat fishing industry moved to mechanized fishing vessels and the import of trawlers. The British and American occupation of Iceland during World War II injected money into the Icelandic economy, launching various projects and raising wages. In the early 2000s, it built a great deal of wealth in the banking industry. In the fourth quarter of 2008, the worldwide recession hit and Iceland's banking industry, its stock market, and its currency (the krona), all plummeted. The country had high unemployment, high debt, and high inflation.

Iceland became international news in April 2010, when the eruption of volcano Eyjafjallajökull shut down European air traffic for a week. The volcano Grímsvötn did the same thing for three days the following year. The international attention on Iceland coincided with the country expanding its airline routes to and through the country. Tourism to Iceland boomed, making it a faster-growing destination than any place in Europe.

Tourist visits increased 440 percent in the seven years following the 2010 eruption. That industry was disrupted in 2020 by the COVID-19 pandemic. At the start of the 2021 tourist season, the Fagradalsfjall volcano became active with multiple cones of fountaining lava, filling a valley less than an hour's drive from Reykjavík with miles of flowing lava. Hundreds of thousands of people came to Iceland that year to see the active volcano.

AN ISLAND IN THE North Atlantic, Iceland has a long history of fishing. This history includes stories of many people who made a living by fishing—and then drowning. That is because earlier generations learned to fish, but they never learned to swim.

Today, learning to swim is obligatory in Iceland. In every town you'll find the social center of the community: a soccer field next to a playground, next to a basketball court, next to the community pool. Icelanders will show up at the same time each day, hang their clothes on the same hook in the locker room, and sit with the same neighbors in the pool. Scandinavians have their saunas. Wisconsin has its roadside taverns. The community pool is the social gathering place for Icelanders. There are more than one hundred heated community pools in Iceland.

We were told that no matter what time of year you go to Iceland, be prepared to get wet. We made sure to pack a couple of different rain jackets, rain pants, a swimsuit, and a stocking cap. We dressed in layers. We got wet from wind and rain and waterfalls. We got wet and warm sitting in geyser-heated pools.

Icelanders open their screenless windows in their homes and

apartments almost all the time. They even open their front doors, even in winter. Icelanders love fresh air. Visitors to Iceland will love it as well. People can afford to open the windows in winter because Iceland's heating costs are so low. The island's electricity leaves virtually no carbon footprint as it is generated by geothermal, hydroelectric, or wind sources. Iceland is also a safe country. You will see babies left in carriages outside a store while their parents go in to shop. Icelanders prefer to leave their babies outside in the fresh air.

My spouse and I expected to be at the summer Olympics in Japan, sitting with tens of thousands of others in a newly constructed stadium. Instead, we found ourselves soaking in a riverway warmed by the earth's geothermal activity. We expected to be in the most populated city on earth, but instead we went hiking on some of the newest and most unsettled terrain on the planet. It reminded us to embrace the wonderful wrong turns and happy accidents of travel.

04

BRINGING IT ALL BACK HOME

Chapter 15

GO NAVY

Pensacola

I HAVE BEEN INVITED to travel to places that were never on my radar. I would have to go to a map to see where they were at. I have discovered each place can be rich with culture, history, food, topography, and biology.

One day I got a call from the National Naval Aviation Museum, which is on a US Naval Air Station. I had to go look up where it was. It is in Pensacola overlooking the Gulf of Mexico in the panhandle of Florida.

They wanted to expand their museum, build an IMAX theater, and maybe even produce a film for it. They wanted to know if I would be interested in consulting for them. What person living in Minnesota, with its long winters, wouldn't accept an invitation to Pensacola?

When I walked in and met the head of the Museum Foundation, he said, "We know everything about the Navy, but we know nothing about museums. That's why you're here." That person was retired Navy vice admiral Jack Fetterman. Thus began a multi-year consulting opportunity for me, and the beginning of my love for the Gulf of Mexico.

Fetterman did his early training in Pensacola and flew off the aircraft carrier the USS *Essex*. Late in his Navy career, he became the chief of naval education and training. He began developing a training program to instill core values that addressed sexual harassment, racism, and violence in the Navy. During that development, the Tailhook scandal happened. Scores of naval aviation officers were accused of sexually accosting women during the thirty-fifth Annual Tailhook Association Symposium in 1991. The scandal led to the implementation of much-needed changes in the military with respect to policies toward women. Fetterman's course was quickly incorporated as required training at the Naval Academy. In 1993, the secretary of defense revised the policy on female assignment in the military, opening them up to assignments in combat aircraft. Women began to fly Navy fighter planes off aircraft carriers.

After his retirement from the Navy, Jack Fetterman became a visionary in the city of Pensacola, including a role as the head of the foundation that raised the money to grow the Naval Aviation Museum. The foundation built the museum's buildings, restored and displayed naval aircraft, and created business ventures. The Navy maintains the museum facilities, which is why it is the cleanest museum I have ever been in.

Technically, Pensacola is on Pensacola Bay in the Gulf of Mexico, protected by the Fairpoint Peninsula and the forty-mile Santa Rosa Barrier Island beyond. Barrier islands are typically made up of sand dunes formed by waves and tides that run parallel to a coast. The coasts of the Gulf of Mexico are resplendent with barrier islands. Padre Island in Texas is not only the longest on the Gulf, but the longest on Earth. Most barrier islands are part of a chain. There are also barrier islands that connect to the mainland, which is the origin of Fairpoint Peninsula off Pensacola.

On my first trip to Pensacola, home base was a hotel room in a historic building in downtown Pensacola. The hotel's one big shortcoming: it wasn't on the water. As part of my work, I would spend time learning more about the surrounding area of

Pensacola and its tourism trade. That meant I had to head for the water to find a place where I would stay on my future trips to Pensacola. It turned out to be Gulf Breeze, Florida.

Gulf Breeze is located on the Fairpoint Peninsula. To get there, you must take the Pensacola Bay Bridge. The bridge is often called the Three-Mile Bridge, in reference to its length. It is a four-lane roadway that rises more than sixty feet over the beautiful blue water. With its water views, it is one of the most splendid drives I have ever made. The bridge is now operating its third manifestation. The original bridge opened in 1931. It was replaced in 1960. The current iteration opened in 2019 with a pedestrian lane so you can walk or bike across. During the 2020 hurricane season, Hurricane Sally broke a barge loose from its mooring. It got stuck under the bridge and caused a temporary closure. The Gulf Coast and hurricanes have an inseparable history.

Gulf Breeze is immediately over the Pensacola Bay Bridge from Pensacola. There I found a two-story hotel with a half dozen rooms that had lawns leading right to the water. The room on the main floor at the end of this set of rooms was the Hospitality Center, where guests could find free drinks and appetizers for a couple of hours early each evening. One or another of these ground-floor rooms with a grassy beach became my Pensacola home for the many years I spent working with the Naval Aviation Museum.

Farther east on the peninsula is the unincorporated town of Navarre. One State of Florida tourism website reads, "Relaxation is the main attraction in Navarre." The eight-mile stretch of Navarre Beach includes a marine park. Navarre also has the longest fishing pier on the Gulf of Mexico, measuring more than 1,500 feet long. It was rebuilt in 2010 after hurricane damage.

Today, Pensacola is commonly referred to as the Cradle of

Naval Aviation. The US Navy commissioned its first naval air station there in 1914. Every Navy, Marine, and Coast Guard flyer has trained at the Naval Air Station in Pensacola, including John Glenn, the first American to orbit the earth, and Neil Armstrong, the first person to walk on the moon. The Naval Air Station in Pensacola is also home to the Blue Angels, the Navy's flight demonstration team that performs at air shows around the United States.

A staff member from the Naval Aviation Museum gave me my first introduction to Pensacola and its beaches. The Gulf Coast beaches of the panhandle are made up of beautiful white sand. Microscopic quartz crystals have eroded off the Appalachian Mountains, washed down riverways into the Gulf of Mexico, and then washed up onto the shore.

I remember walking the beautiful white sand beaches without encountering any other people, until we came upon a group of three. What struck me was how short they were and how high pitched their voices were. Their dialect was new to me, and they were extremely friendly. It was another moment of the inevitable uncertainty of life. I reminded myself to be respectful of the places you visit and the people you meet. I listened, not questioned. And, after we separated company, I simply asked my colleague who these people were. Politely, my cohort said, "Cajuns."

Cajuns are of Roman Catholic French descent. In the United States, they primarily live on or near the Gulf Coast in Louisiana. The Great Expulsion occurred in the 1750s and 1760s, when the British expelled the Acadian people from their home in the present-day maritime provinces of Canada: Nova Scotia, New Brunswick, and Prince Edward Island. Many migrated to Spanish Louisiana, where the Acadians became "Cajuns."

As Catholics, they follow the customs of the season of Lent, the forty-day period of spiritual reflection and Friday fish fries, that leads up to Easter Sunday. Lent begins on Ash Wednesday. The day before is Shrove Tuesday, or Fat Tuesday, which translates in French to *Mardi Gras*. In a ritual called *Courir de Mardi Gras*, a group on horseback rode from farm to farm to request something for a community jumbo pot. The tradition dates to medieval times in France when the less fortunate would go to the homes of the wealthy and perform for contributions.

I USED TO SNEAK off from my accommodations in Gulf Breeze and drive an hour east on Highway 98 to Destin for dinner. Destin taught me the value of exploring places you never previously had even heard of or read about. In Destin, you can scuba or snorkel to sunken ships, airplanes, barges, and army tanks. These wrecks provide a habitat for numerous fish species, making Destin a mecca for local Gulf of Mexico seafood, including grouper, red snapper, flounder, wahoo, oysters, crab, and Gulf shrimp. Wahoos are popular to fish for because they are a challenge to catch. They are also good eating with white, firm, and flaky flesh.

With more than 340 sunny days per year and an average high temperature of 75°F, Destin's weather is indicative of what Florida's Gulf Coast provides. Let the tourists go to Orlando. Be a traveler and head to the white sand beaches and natural habitats of the Florida panhandle. Enjoy the authentic environment, food, and history.

Traveling east from Destin, you will go through Panama City and Port St. Joe to the twenty-five-mile St. George Island, a barrier island at the mouth of the Apalachicola River, which still carries the grains of quartz down from the Appalachian Mountains, adding to the white sand beaches of the Gulf. With its low-density zoning, St. George Island is a tranquil setting off the Florida panhandle that is well known for its conch fritters and oysters, which are roasted on an open fire on the beach. One of my favorite dinners in the Florida panhandle was marinated mullet and hush puppies, which are small balls of deep-fried cornmeal batter. The tastiest mullet fish is the black mullet from the Gulf of Mexico.

Because oysters filter so much water—more than a gallon an hour—they develop a flavor profile that reflects their environment. You'll find oysters at coastal locations worldwide, but the fresh water of the Mississippi River that runs into the Gulf lowers the salinity of the water, making Gulf Oysters large, tender, and meaty. You can eat them steamed, fried, or baked. To best discern their range of flavor—from briny, buttery, sweet, and mild—you eat them cold on the half shell.

ONE AFTERNOON WHEN I was in the office of Rear Admiral Fetterman, he asked, "What day is it?" I reminded him it was Monday. "That means tomorrow, the Blue Angels will practice," he said.

The Blue Angels are a precision flying demonstration team. The jets are piloted by Navy and Marine Corps jet pilots with aircraft carrier qualifications and a minimum of 1,250 hours of flying Navy tactical jets. They were established after World War II to raise interest in naval aviation. In the 1960s, they flew F-4 Phantoms. They transitioned to A-4 Skyhawks in 1974 and, in 1986, they began flying Boeing F/A-18 Hornets. Pilots serve two years with the team and then return to their squadrons.

During the air show season, which runs April through October, the Blue Angels fly to cities around the United States and provide the finale to weekend air shows with their precision jet flying demonstration. They return to their base, the Pensacola Naval Air Station, between air shows. Every Tuesday morning, weather permitting, they practice.

Admiral Fetterman told me where to go, where to park, what time to get there, and what gate to walk through to watch the practice. Hoping to look the part, I wore a blue suit and put on aviator sunglasses as I parked my rental car and walked through the appointed cyclone fence gate the next morning.

I walked toward the flight line with a hangar alongside it. An airman approached me. "You will need these, sir," he said, as he handed me earplugs. I found a single set of metal bleachers, like you would find at a little league baseball field, along the flight line with a dozen spectators seated on it. We were closer to the runway than you would ever be allowed at an air show. It was as though we had been invited to a private performance by the Blue Angels.

I returned to the museum after watching the Blue Angels practice and suggested to Admiral Fetterman: they should allow—even encourage—the public to park in the museum's lot on Tuesday mornings where they could watch the Blue Angels for free. It could attract a lot of visitors, who then would naturally come to the museum. Today, the National Naval Aviation Museum hosts open bleacher seating for one thousand people. Chairs can be rented. Concessions and merchandise are available. (National security and public health considerations can impact access to the Naval Air Station and the museum, so visitors should check well in advance before planning a visit.)

Admiral Fetterman had a vision of expanding the museum to include an IMAX theater and producing a film on the Blue Angels. The expanded museum would feature a display of restored Blue Angel A-4 Skyhawks in formation hanging from its central atrium, along with a National Flight Academy for seventh through twelfth graders that was modeled after Space Camp at the Space and Rocket Center in Huntsville, Alabama. All his visions came to fruition at the National Naval Aviation Museum.

Pensacola's minor league baseball team is the Blue Wahoos. They play at Fetterman Field.

Chapter 16

THE GREAT AMERICAN ECLIPSE

Nebraska

THE MOTTO OF THE United States Marine Corps is "Semper Fidelis," which is Latin and means "Always Faithful." I had a sign in my office that was a variation on that. It said "Semper Gumby."

Gumby and Pokey are claymation figures, which premiered on television in the 1950s. Gumby is a green humanoid figure and Pokey is his sidekick, a talking orange pony. I remember Gumby being able to roll up like a ball to accelerate his movement forward. I had a little rubber Gumby in my office under the sign that said "Semper Gumby." It means "Always Flexible." This motto has served me well throughout my worldwide travels. It is especially key if you want to successfully see a total solar eclipse.

On August 27, 2017, a solar eclipse was visible across the entire contiguous United States, the first to cross the whole of the country in ninety-nine years. It was dubbed "The Great American Eclipse." Those fortunate enough to be in the path of the moon's shadow under clear skies can say they saw a "total eclipse of the sun." Those outside the path of totality saw a "partial" eclipse. Anyone who has witnessed both can say the difference between a total and partial eclipse is like the difference between making mad passionate love compared to having your grandmother kiss you on the cheek. There is no comparison.

The moon casts a shadow that extends into space, and on the rare occasion when the sun, Earth, and moon are in the right alignment, the moon's shadow moves across the Earth in a narrow path. During the Great American Eclipse, the moon's shadow traveled from the coast of Oregon to the coast of South Carolina, racing from west to east for 2,500 miles in ninety minutes. The moon's shadow was a mere seventy miles wide. The length of time anybody in the shadow path experienced a total eclipse was less than three minutes.

The moon's shadow doesn't pick a path across the surface of the Earth in consideration of human access or accommodations. You must be flexible as to when and where you go to see an eclipse. Total eclipses don't come to you. You have to go to them. And even after you pick a spot that the shadow of the moon will pass over, you may have to go somewhere else, far or fast, if the weather is going to interfere with your viewing of the eclipse.

THE GREAT AMERICAN ECLIPSE was my fifth total eclipse of the sun. The previous four all required I travel outside of the United States. It was only well after my first total solar eclipse experience that I realized how lucky I was. With a gang of school buddies, I took a summer road trip from Chicago up through Maine and into the Maritime Provinces of Canada. We slept in youth hostel tents and watched the eclipse from a sand dune on the shore of Prince Edward Island. I brought one piece of welder's glass, and we all shared it to view the partial phases. We had two minutes and five seconds of totality and clear skies, which was lucky. But the real luck was not bringing cameras or telescopes, which we certainly couldn't afford at the time. They would have distracted us from simply experiencing the eclipse. The other thing I learned was that the best location for eclipse viewing is out in the open, ideally amid a natural unspoiled environment, away from civilization and its buildings.

I chose Kearney, Nebraska, as my base for the 2017 Great American Eclipse, because I could drive along Interstate 80 130 miles east to Lincoln, or 100 miles west to North Platte, and be in the path of the moon's shadow. The day before the eclipse I drove those distances on I-80, and highways north and south, in anticipation of being flexible to do so on eclipse day. If clouds or rain were to move in on my preferred eclipse viewing site near Kearney, I had to be ready to run—Semper Gumby.

Thanks to the weather on eclipse day, I didn't have to "chase" the eclipse. I successfully experienced what my eclipse app told me was two minutes and thirty-three seconds of totality at the Crane Trust property—ten thousand acres along the Platte River, forty miles east of Kearney, a place through which, in early spring, sandhill cranes migrate. (On March 19, 2019, 326,000 cranes passed through, plus or minus 72,000, according to the official count.)

Of the five total solar eclipses I have traveled to see, I have only been clouded out once. That was on an eclipse trip to Colombia for what was to be fifty seconds of totality. A group of avid astronomy enthusiasts arranged a trip to Bogotá, Colombia, where we boarded a bus that took us east over the Andes Mountains to the little town of Aqua Azul. Conveniently the eclipse happened on a national holiday, *Día de la Raza*, the Day of the Race (what we once referred to in the United States as Columbus Day). The holiday fell on a Monday, which meant school in Aqua Azul was closed that day. Our group rented the school, a series of cinder block buildings, where we slept on the concrete floors on Saturday, Sunday, and Monday nights. We packed up and headed out early the next morning in time for school to resume.

The eclipse took place late on that Monday, with the sun low in the west. Rain clouds blocked our view of the sun. Semper Gumby—three of us jumped in a jeep and headed east, hoping we could catch a view of the sun above the clouds. But, to no avail. When we stopped the jeep at the moment of totality, with rain clouds along the western horizon, we noticed a rainbow to the east. James Westlake, a fellow traveler from Louisiana, wrote in *Sky & Telescope* magazine, "We watched in awe as the rainbow was devoured by the lunar shadow." Though we were clouded out from seeing the sun eclipsed, we did experience something that only the group of us assembled there ever reported seeing in the history of humanity: what happens to a rainbow during a total solar eclipse. The rainbow that faded out as the total eclipse arrived snapped back to brilliance fifty seconds later.

KEARNEY, NEBRASKA, HAD NOT been in the path of a total eclipse in 823 years, and following the 2017 Great American Eclipse, another one would not happen there for 727 years. My base camp was a motel with a buffet breakfast starting at 5:00 a.m. There was one other person in the breakfast room with me in that hour. He filled his plate with four biscuits, which he covered in gravy. Then, out of his backpack, he pulled a bottle of Great Value Louisiana Hot Sauce and drizzled it on top. Biscuits and gravy didn't appeal to me as an eclipse day first meal, so I ate light and stopped at a Caribou Coffee in the neighborhood that opened at 6:00 a.m. I ordered two large, iced coffees, each with a shot of espresso, to go. I arrived at the Crane Trust visitor center in the 7:00 a.m. hour and purposely parked my car facing out near the entryway, in case I had to make a weather run. Fortunately, a colleague of mine, Mike Augustyniak, the director of meteorology for CBS TV in Minneapolis, was based that day in Lincoln, Nebraska. He kept me informed of weather developments via text messages.

Another cohort, who was stationed in Casper, Wyoming, for the eclipse, had stopped at the Crane Center and scouted it for me a week prior. A good piece of advice accompanied a picture of his spouse wearing shorts and sandals and smiling in sunshine on one of the tall grass prairie trails. She reported she got chiggers. It taught me to wear my leather hiking boots, long pants, and DEET to scout the Crane Trust property on Saturday, August 25—two days before the eclipse—on my way from overnighting in Des Moines, Iowa, heading to Kearney. I took pictures and made notes on where the sun was in the sky exactly forty-eight hours before totality. This was to help me decide on where I wanted to be when the eclipse happened two days later.

FOLLOWING THE GREAT AMERICAN ECLIPSE in 2017, I loved reading reports from first-time eclipse viewers. One of my favorites was from Jim Hoffman, CNET staff member, who lived in Oregon, just outside of the eclipse shadow path. He and his wife traveled into the path of the shadow where they got fifty-five seconds of totality. He wrote, "The town we live in, Dundee, lays about a mile outside that zone, so we decided it would be well worth the effort to get ourselves underneath that shadow. Turns out it would have been worth it even if we'd been forced to trek across a barren desert or frozen tundra via arthritic sled dogs. I'd read in days leading up to the eclipse that totality is ten thousand times more spectacular than just seeing 99 percent, and now I know why. Totality is just that: the total experience."

What was my fourth total eclipse of the sun was David Makepeace's first on July 11, 1991, under cloudless skies on

Mexico's Baja Peninsula. "It was as if our little spot on Earth had fallen out of time," he wrote on his website eclipseguy.com. "It was as if we had been arrested in a dome of dark sky so the universe could peer in at us with its one giant eye to see if we were paying attention." He has since become a hardcore eclipse chaser, joining one of the most compulsive of subcultures, and chasing more than twenty eclipses including to Libya, Patagonia, Aruba, and China. "Get your ass to totality," he wrote. "Quit wasting your life."

AN HOUR BEFORE TOTALITY for the 2017 event, I exchanged a final text with my meteorologist cohort. His text told me to stay in place at the Crane Trust property, as I would find scattered high cirrus clouds no matter which way, or how far, I went in the final hour. At that point I put on my hiking boots and my bug spray and put my folded camp chair and backpack over my shoulder to begin my hike from the Crane Trust parking lot. I made one last stop in the bathroom in the visitor center and then headed out to the pedestrian bridges across the Platte River and onto the vast tall grass prairie acreage. Most of the crowd there stayed close to the building, which gave me the opportunity to hike to an isolated spot along the grass trails. I was able to stay within earshot of the crowd, which I discovered at my first eclipse, is part of the experience.

As most of the people assembled with us in Nebraska were eclipse virgins, I stopped along the hike out to my viewing spot to encourage people to take off those silly paper eclipse glasses they were wearing for the last hour before totality. I also encouraged people who, like myself, were wearing sunglasses to take them off for that same final hour. This was so they could witness the illumination changes that would take place at an accelerated pace in the waning minutes before totality. I had first learned this when three of us hiked to an isolated sand dune on the shores of Prince Edward Island for my virgin eclipse experience.

In Nebraska I noticed dramatic illumination change about fifteen minutes before totality, and when it became pronounced, I looked at my timepiece to note it was seven minutes before totality. There was a dimness to the sunlight unlike any dawn or dusk I had ever known. I looked around at my shadow on the mowed grass and the tree line beyond along the Platte River. It all appeared to be sharper in focus than I had ever experienced, like I had some super vision. And the color of the grass and trees was foreign to me. I sensed the irregularity of what I was experiencing. I asked myself, "Am I dreaming?"

I have always contended that this illumination change during an eclipse is completely foreign to us as humans. It's something we have not experienced during our millions of years of evolution, since we split off from those that became chimpanzees. Our eye-mind system can only regard it as alien. It is as though we have been transported to another world where, in a matter of minutes, totality will begin and the space we are occupying will, with the snap of a finger, become even more extraordinary.

This experience has scientific explanation. While it provides interesting background into the physiology of the eye, it doesn't extend to what is happening in your brain as you experience—and try and make sense of—the unique illumination changes of a total solar eclipse.

Stuart Mangel, a professor of neuroscience at the Ohio State University College of Medicine, was in Tennessee for the August 21, 2017, eclipse. As reported in *Ohio State News*, "He and others experienced an unusual clarity of vision." Mangel said, "During the total eclipse, it was as dark as it usually is at dusk. Several people I was with commented that they could see as well during totality as they could when it had been bright, and that their acuity was much better than it usually is when it is dark at dusk." According to the article:

> He realized at the time that his research offers one explanation.
>
> Normally, when you're outdoors, it takes hours for the background light to decrease from bright to dark as the Earth rotates on its axis. When it finally becomes dark at dusk, a person or animal's ability to see small details is much lower than during the middle of the day.
>
> Visual performance needs change with the ambient light level, Mangel said. We need to see fine spatial details on bright days and to see large dim objects on moonless nights.

Mangel was the lead on a team of researchers who found out why this happened at the biological level. Their explanation was based on "the presence (or absence) of a protein in the retina known as a GABA receptor." According to Mangel:

> GABA, short for gamma-aminobutyric acid, is a chemical messenger responsible for communication between cells, especially those in the brain.
>
> The GABA receptor is in abundance on certain cells in the retina on sunny days and enhances the ability to see details and edges of objects. At night, it disappears.
>
> But that process is normally gradual. When the total eclipse took viewers from brightness to darkness in minutes, the GABA receptor would have still been present on those cells in their eyes, giving them super-sharp vision for a brief time.

This explanation gave me a deeper understanding of what I'd experienced during the eclipse, and why it affected me so profoundly. As Mangel put it:

"Evolution has made trade-offs so that we can see well on bright days *and* on moonless nights," he said. "My findings show that the change in background light triggers a process in the retina that normally takes hours. [. . .] The reason our acuity stayed high during the total eclipse is that there wasn't enough time for protein disassembly to take place."

My scouting of the Crane Trust property two days in advance of the eclipse allowed me to pick a position and know where the sun would be in the sky come totality. As I stood alone on the edge of the tall grass prairie in the heat and humidity of an August afternoon in Nebraska, I noted how noisy it was. There was a loud and constant buzzing and clicking of insects in the tall grass, a cacophony from a population of critters I didn't know and couldn't see as I stood among them under the bright sun.

So, two days later, on a gorgeous afternoon for a total eclipse, I sat in my camp chair within earshot of the crowds of people who had made the Crane property their eclipse viewing site. I do not film, photograph, or record data, and I don't wear eclipse glasses to watch the partial phases. I am there to experience it.

During totality, I went through a mental checklist of what I should look for. Oh, turn all the way around to observe what is a 360-degree sunset effect on the horizon. And scan the whole sky to see if any stars can be spotted. Other than the eclipsed sun, the only other object I saw was the planet Venus. For my entire life I have only seen Venus, which is always close to the sun in the sky, as the evening star or the morning star. This is the first time I have ever seen it as the 1:00 p.m. star.

During totality, I sensed something I never anticipated. There were bursts of a breeze leading up to totality, noticeable because it was refreshingly cooling in the August midday heat in Nebraska. During totality, there was no breeze. But the most surprising thing of all? It went silent.

Was I dreaming? Had I gone deaf? Should I believe that this space ballet had, for mere minutes, hypnotized living creatures—including myself—in the shadow of the moon?

Enter Andy Caven, biologist at the Crane Trust property. On eclipse day I met him and asked him what insects I was hearing in the tall grass prairie standing alone on my scouting trip two days before. He said they were cicadas, leaf hoppers, and short-horned and pygmy grasshoppers, whose populations are high in August. I emailed Andy after the eclipse to ask if he or any of the Crane staff had the same experience as I did with silence. I was excited when his response was, "We quantified the experience."

Months later he shared his article, "Assessing biological and environmental effects of a total solar eclipse with passive multimodal technologies." It was published by Andy, along with principals from the Department of Forestry and Natural Resources at Purdue University, the Center for Global Soundscapes at Purdue, the Department of Biology at the University of Nebraska–Kearney, and the Department of Agricultural Leadership, Education, and Communication at the University of Nebraska–Lincoln.

On the day of the eclipse they photographed common and prairie sunflowers, morning glories, and moon flowers to see if there would be any flowering response during the eclipse: none recorded.

Motion-triggered cameras on game trails and in bat roosts recorded any wildlife movement: none recorded.

Then, there was the acoustical record. "At the onset of totality, sounds of howling, cheering, and yelling, ranging from five to fifteen seconds, were recorded from people congregated in the path of totality." And "sounds of wind through dry, late summer vegetation, generally decreased about an hour before, quieted during, and restarted about an hour after totality." And the most extraordinary data recorded: "Calls of cicada . . . ground cricket calls . . . ceased during eclipse coverage."

At a time and place that might typically be regarded as an ordinary August day in Nebraska, I had experienced an extraordinary moment in the history of the cosmos. I can bear witness. The tall grass critters going completely silent for the mere minutes of the total eclipse had really happened.

Chapter 17

STORM CHASING

TORNADO ALLEY

LONG BEFORE I MET tornado chasers, I met volcano chasers. I spent seven years with filmmaker, documentarian, and volcano chaser George Casey doing a giant screen film on the Pacific Basin *Ring of Fire*. When you spend seven years working and traveling with someone on a project, you get to know them and their family. I watched George Casey's kids grow up. So, what does the son of a volcano chaser grow up to be? George's oldest son, Sean, became a tornado chaser.

Sean Casey decided he was not just going to chase tornadoes and film them in IMAX. He committed to getting hit by a tornado with his camera running. To do so, he built the Tornado Intercept Vehicle—the TIV. He started with a Ford turbodiesel truck frame and engine, around which he built an armor-plated vehicle with bullet resistant windows. One of the dangers of tornadoes is the uplift they create, so the TIV had armor plates that, with the help of hydraulics, slid down each side of the vehicle and staked into the ground with steel spikes. The TIV chased a tornado to get ahead of it, then anchored itself to the ground at the anticipated touchdown site. The TIV had a turret on top that housed an IMAX camera that could turn around 360°.

Sean Casey and the TIV dedicated each spring for several years to chase tornadoes in Tornado Alley. This is a region of the United States where, during May and June, frequent tornadoes and severe storms can take place. The region runs north to south from the Canadian border to the Mexico border, and from the Rocky Mountains on the west to the Mississippi River on the east. Tornadoes occur east of the Mississippi, and the southeast United States is an extension of Tornado Alley with long tracking and destructive tornadoes. However, storm chasers don't like to travel east of the Mississippi because of all the trees. These can be quite dangerous as flying projectiles in a severe storm. Storm chasers see a lot of Oklahoma, Kansas, and Nebraska.

Sean Casey was featured on the Discovery Channel's *Stormchasers* TV show. After accumulating years' worth of tornado-chasing footage, in 2009 the TIV joined the largest assemblage of severe storm researchers ever coordinated. The project was called VORTEX, for the Verification of the Origins of Rotation in Tornadoes Experiment. VORTEX represented the first time scientists researched the entire evolution of a tornado in conjunction with so many instruments. The first VORTEX project was conducted in the spring of 1994. The second project, VORTEX2, was conducted in 2009 and 2010.

The VORTEX2 fleet had one hundred scientists in more than forty vehicles in a nomadic two-month chase of tornadoes in May and June in Tornado Alley. The vehicles included a Doppler on Wheels mounted on a semi flatbed truck, as well as more than a dozen radar instruments, and more than three dozen deployable instruments like weather balloons and unmanned flying craft.

I had agreed to participate in the financing of Sean Casey's project to do a giant screen film on tornadoes. In early June 2010, the producer of the film and I joined the VORTEX group. The tornado-chasing project had no home base; it required a nomadic lifestyle. Every morning, the principal scientists would meet at 9:00 a.m. to review what had happened in the days before and make decisions based upon forecasts ahead. At 10:00 a.m. the entire VORTEX team would meet, along with a myriad of people, like myself, who could best be described as hangers-on. The week we joined the group, there was a Japanese TV crew, and a troop of Boy Scouts, joining the escapade.

The full-group briefing ended with the weather forecast ahead and the team leaders' decision about what to do next. The team would provide a meeting location for 3:00 p.m., which was a typical start on any given day of severe weather. The fleet would drive into a severe weather cell and move with it until dark. The chase was always called off at dusk as it was too dangerous to drive in severe storms after dark. At that point the team would learn where they would be spending the night.

The day the film producer and I were scheduled to join the VORTEX caravan we caught a morning flight from Midway airport in Chicago to Denver, where we would rent a car and expect a call to tell us where to drive. Flying from Chicago to Denver allowed us to pick up an hour, as we were moving from the central time zone to the mountain time zone. At the rental car company, the agent asked what kind of vehicle we wanted. My colleague and I had not discussed this level of detail for our trip and we both stood there mute, wondering if we were supposed to rent a fast vehicle or a big vehicle, or something in between. The only instructions the tornado team had given us: make sure to take out full insurance on a rented car, and don't tell anyone at the rental company what we would be doing with their vehicle. We decided on big and rented a white Chevy Suburban.

Our crew instructed us to drive north from Denver to Cheyenne, Wyoming, a little more than a ninety-minute trip. From there, we took the crew's directions to the state highway east under darkening skies. Then, suddenly, we encountered the VORTEX team coming in the opposite direction—scores of vehicles flashing by us, heading the other way. Our decision making at that point was easy: we turned around and followed the caravan of vehicles.

After a high-speed drive, the team turned onto a small roadway and pulled into a grammar school parking lot. Dark clouds swirled overhead and everyone stood outside of their vehicles looking skyward. One of the team members standing on the back of the flatbed holding the large Doppler dish cried out, "Everybody in your vehicle—one minute to hail!" We hopped into our vehicle and within a minute, the largest, loudest hail I had ever experienced pounded down. We dropped to the floorboards, one of us on top of the other. Then we realized you shouldn't park your vehicle at a right angle to the storm direction. We should have parked with our back end toward the approaching storm to risk only the back windows being hit directly by hail. When the hail stopped we had no broken windows, but our vehicle looked like a dimpled golf ball.

After a few hours we got a call that we would be spending the night in Chadron, Nebraska, another couple of hours ahead. This was the routine of storm chasing. You start each day not knowing where you will spend the night.

A room at the motel in Chadron cost $30 a night. Small animal skulls and dreamcatchers hung on the wall behind the woman working the front desk. In Native American culture, when hung over a bed or crib, a dreamcatcher is a protective charm, a "dream snare." It is a handmade wooden hoop with webbing that forms a net, including sacred feathers or beads.

The Chadron motel desk clerk informed us that there was a back door in our rooms that led into a hallway. At the end of that hallway, we would find free coffee in the morning. After entering my room, I did open the back door and stuck my head into the hallway. The walls, doors from other rooms, and all the door frames were painted the same pea green color under dim flickering florescent illumination. I looked down the empty hall that appeared to lead to another hallway at the end. There was no sign of a coffee maker, or any furniture or wall hangings in this corridor. I shut the door, locked it, and never dared to venture down it. I thought about going back to the office to borrow a dreamcatcher to hang over my bed for the night.

I did leave my front door open as I unpacked for our single night in Chadron. A thunderstorm we had been driving through for hours continued. The lightning and sounds of thunder and pouring rain provided a terrific evening show.

At the end of the VORTEX team meeting the next morning, we learned that we would meet at a truck stop along Interstate 80 near Sidney, Nebraska, 130 miles to the south. At 3:00 p.m., the fleet parked at a truck stop to grab snack food and microwaved breakfast or lunch sandwiches. If you can't make truck stop and fast food part of your diet, you will starve as a storm chaser.

It was a waiting game at the truck stop. After weeks of storm chasing, it seemed as though each team member had become something of an expert with respect to the enterprise. On this day, the expert was a still photographer documenting the project. After more than an hour of waiting she said nothing was going to happen and she was going to take her laundry into the truck stop and do a couple of loads. Halfway through the wash cycle, the team leaders hollered to everyone, "Saddle up, we are heading south to Colorado in ten minutes." She ran into the truck stop, brought out her loads of wet clothes, and threw them into her vehicle. Semper Gumby.

Following my experience with the IMAX and VORTEX crews, I came home and went online, where you can find commercial operators that will take you on storm-chasing tours. They generally start from Denver or Oklahoma City during the spring. I asked my spouse if she would like to join me on such a tour. She said she did not regard that as a proper invitation for a date. I still have it on my wish list to return to Tornado Alley on one of these tours. Some of the weeklong trips have names like "May Mayhem," "Wicked Weather," and "Flying Cow" tours.

The first year of the VORTEX project was the inspiration for the 1996 Hollywood film *Twister*, which starred Bill Paxton. He served as the narrator for our IMAX film, *Tornado Alley*. It included outstanding footage of a tornado moving down a roadway right behind the TIV and the vehicle being engulfed by the swirling winds.

I grew up in the United States in Illinois. I was used to summer thunderstorms, lightning, and hail. I remember going into the basement when the severe storm sirens went off. But that experience did not prepare me for being in Tornado Alley during the severe storm season. These storms were a tremendous magnification of what I had known. Spending afternoons until dark speeding across the great plains of the United States under the darkest clouds and most powerful storms I had ever experienced was certainly dangerous but, nonetheless, an experience that felt otherworldly, even for a midwestern guy.

Chapter 18

CONSERVATION COUNTRY

WISCONSIN

ON A BIKE RIDE on a hot summer day in southwest Wisconsin, my bride and I rode past a farmstead where three young children were doing chores in the front yard. One girl, the tallest and oldest of the three, was barefoot behind a push lawn mower. The others, whom we assumed were her brother and sister, raked up the grass clippings. As we approached, they all stopped, stiffened, and stared. They never took their wide eyes off us as we rode past. "Those kids looked at us like we are aliens," I said to my spouse when we came to a stop. My bride replied, "Look at us. We're in shorts, I'm wearing a halter top. You are shirtless. We have on helmets, sunglasses, and we are riding $500 Trek bikes. We *are* aliens." There were no electrical lines leading to the farmstead, and the children all had on long sleeves, pants, and the boy was in a straw hat. It was apparent they were Amish.

The bicycle ride instilled in me an appetite to learn more about the Amish. With hopes of visiting them in person, I reminded myself of important travel lessons I'd learned: be respectful of the people you meet and get creative about connecting.

The Amish originated from a Christian religious split in Switzerland late in the seventeenth century. In the early eighteenth century, they began migrating to America, settling in Pennsylvania. Their homes have no electricity, and their toilets are in an outhouse. They travel in horse-drawn buggies, and they speak in a German dialect. Their church districts have between twenty and forty families, and they hold worship services every other Sunday in a member's home. Each district is led by a bishop. Today, almost all the world's Amish live in the United States, and they are concentrated in the Midwest, from Pennsylvania to Missouri.

Until the 1950s, almost all Amish children attended small, local, non-Amish schools. But public school consolidation and mandatory schooling beyond eighth grade caused Amish opposition. In 1972, three Amish students stopped attending high school in New Glarus in Green County, Wisconsin. Under the Wisconsin Compulsory School Attendance Law, they faced $5 fines in county court. The court found that the requirement of high school attendance until age sixteen was a "reasonable" exercise of governmental power. A Wisconsin circuit court affirmed the decision, but the Wisconsin Supreme Court found in favor of the Amish. The US Supreme Court upheld the decision, finding that:

> Amish objection to formal education beyond the eighth grade is firmly grounded in central religious concepts. They object to high school . . . because the values they teach are in marked variance with Amish values and the Amish way of life. The high school tends to emphasize intellectual and scientific accomplishments, self-distinction, competitiveness, worldly success, and social life with other students. Amish society emphasizes informal learning-through-doing; a life of "goodness," rather than a life of intellect; wisdom, rather than technical knowledge; community welfare, rather

than competition; and separation from, rather than integration with, contemporary worldly society.

Since the Supreme Court's decision, Amish children rarely attend formal education past eighth grade, and they are educated in one-room schoolhouses by teachers who are young, unmarried women from the Amish community.

Non-Amish people are referred to as "English." There is a veil between the "English" and the Amish that makes it hard to get to know them. They have always intrigued me but, even after many trips in Amish country, they remain an enigma.

On another summer bike trip, my spouse and I spent a weekend in one of the more than two dozen highly rated bed and breakfasts in historic homes and inns in Lanesboro, Minnesota. Lanesboro and the town of Harmony are in the southeast corner of Minnesota, near the borders with Wisconsin and Iowa. In this part of the world, you can learn more about the Amish, and to deepen my personal curiosity we took advantage of a tour with an "English" member of the community who coordinates with the Amish for visits.

We signed on for a van tour with six other people. To be respectful of the Amish way of life, I wore long sleeves, as they do, even in the summer heat. I didn't wear any jewelry other than my wedding ring. I would respect their wishes to not be photographed; the Amish don't take or keep pictures, as they reject pride and arrogance. As Christians whose sacred text is the Bible, they follow what is written in the Book of James, Chapter 4; "God resisteth the proud, but giveth grace unto the humble." Handmade Amish dolls, which you can buy when you are in Amish country, have no facial features. As the second commandment says, "Thou shalt not make unto thee any graven image."

On our van tour through Amish country, there was a couple who didn't share my awareness of, and respect for, Amish values. They made no effort to get creative about connecting. The couple wore shorts and T-shirts, along with lots of jewelry, perfume, and aftershave. They brought their dog, which proved to be an attraction with the children on the farmsteads we stopped at. This gave the touring couple a lot of opportunities to take pictures of Amish kids. At one point, one of these fellow tourists asked, "Wouldn't it be nice to live such a simple life?" I gave thought to six days a week of manual labor, living without electricity and running water, chopping wood, growing and storing your own food, working and cooking indoors in long pants and long sleeves on a hot summer day, and going to the outhouse during a winter night. That was as far from a simple lifestyle as I could imagine.

During our tour, I did perceive that, like the rest of us in the world, there are Amish who achieve more, while others less. One of our tour stops was to a farmstead with the largest garden and the most well-maintained house and barn on our route. This stop had public toilets. They were in outhouses, but there was a ceramic sink and urinal in the men's room. There was a barrel mounted above the south side of the outhouses. It was painted black and provided gravity-fed, sun-warmed water to the bathroom sink. The centerpiece of the visit to this farmstead was the building that served as a bakery. It was staffed by more than half a dozen women who sold a lot of baked and canned goods, and faceless dolls, to our group. I assumed this farmstead was the most enterprising in the region with respect to its partnerships with tour organizers, and I suspected it had afforded the family more than their Amish neighbors. It was the only bathroom stop on the tour.

Another farmstead specialized in leather goods. We all bought a new belt, wallet, or purse. Nobody bought a saddle for riding a horse, but we could have commissioned one. This place also had a building that was built into the ground on the

CONSERVATION COUNTRY

shady side of a barn. We learned it was an icehouse. This Amish family had cornered the leather and ice business in the territory.

THE LAST ICE AGE flattened much of the American Midwest and left behind silt for what is now the great corn belt of Iowa, Illinois, and Indiana. The last ice age lobed around twenty-four thousand square miles, leaving a different landscape of thousand-foot-high forested plateaus and bluffs above ridges carved by streams and rivers. Roadways are not laid out in a traditional east-west or north-south configuration, because they must follow the stream beds and river valleys that cut deeply through the terrain. This vast region is called the Driftless Area. My experiences with the topography and cultures that the last glacier missed have led me to call it conservation country.

Bisecting the Driftless Area is a 300-mile section of the 2,300-mile-long Mississippi River. Here you will find river settlements with their own history, including Winona, Minnesota; Prairie du Chien, Wisconsin; Dubuque, Iowa; and Galena, Illinois. The Driftless is a rural region with no formal boundaries or borders. It extends into northeast Iowa and northwest Illinois, but most of it is in southwest Wisconsin. The landscape doesn't allow for the extensive row cropping you'll find in Iowa and Illinois, but it does support dairy farming. Seventy-five percent of the raw-milk craft cheese made in Wisconsin comes from the Driftless Area. It is home to Organic Valley, the nation's largest organic dairy cooperative. All their products, including milk, butter, and cheese, are always made on family farms without the use of pesticides, synthetic hormones, or antibiotics.

ALDO LEOPOLD LIVED IN the Driftless Area of Wisconsin from 1924 until the end of his life. He wrote, "There are two spiritual dangers in not owning a farm. One is the danger of supposing that breakfast comes from the grocery. The other that heat comes from the furnace." He had assembled an almanac of his observations of the seasons at his farmstead, along with essays on ecology and ethics, under the title *Great Possessions*. He hoped to have it published as a book, but it was rejected by several publishers who didn't think there was a readership for his writing with a conservation ethic. Leopold wrote, "When we see land as a community to which we belong, we may begin to use it with respect."

Early in 1948, only days before he died fighting a grass fire where he lived, Oxford University Press agreed to publish Leopold's work. The book was published in 1949 under the title *A Sand County Almanac*. It became enormously popular. A paperback release of the book coincided with the environmental movement of the late 1960s. The book has now been translated into fourteen languages.

There is no Sand County in Wisconsin. Leopold lived in Sauk County in the Driftless. The book title was a reference to the sandy soil of the region.

IN SAUK COUNTY, YOU'LL find the International Crane Foundation, the only place on Earth where you can see all fifteen species of cranes found around the world. The 250-acre property is dedicated to the worldwide preservation of cranes and their habitat. There is a visitor center, breeding facilities, and a research library.

George Archibald and Ron Sauey were ornithology students together at Cornell University. They had a vision for the study and preservation of cranes. Following their college graduation in 1973, the Sauey family rented their farm in Sauk County, Wisconsin, to George and Ron for $1. There, the International

CONSERVATION COUNTRY

Crane Foundation began. Today it has almost one hundred staff who collaborate with colleagues in more than fifty countries.

The International Crane Foundation has been an active partner in saving the largest bird in North America, the whooping crane. An adult whooping crane stands five feet tall, with snowy white feathers and black wing tips. It has a black triangular mask across its face and a red patch on its forehead. In 1941, twenty-one known individuals lived in the wild, plus two birds in captivity. The wild birds were in a single migrating group, spending winters on the Gulf Coast of Texas and migrating north for the summer to nest and reproduce in Alberta. They had almost gone extinct, due to habitat loss and intense hunting in the late 1800s and early 1900s.

In the 1800s, there was a population of whooping cranes that migrated south from the Driftless Area of Wisconsin. In 1998, a partnership of numerous conservation and government groups began a program to reestablish a migratory group in that historic flyway. This was at a time when conservation efforts helped the number of wild whooping cranes in the Texas–Alberta group to grow to more than 250.

The United States and Canada partnered to begin a captive breeding program. It started with crane eggs that were collected in Alberta and sent to the Patuxent Wildlife Research Center in Maryland. In 2001, young cranes hatched at Patuxent were moved to the Necedah National Wildlife Refuge in the Driftless Area of Wisconsin. Staff wearing crane costumes reared them, so they did not imprint to humans. A staff member on the whooping crane team at the International Crane Foundation said, "The cranes never see a human face, or hand, or leg. That's because project researchers all wear crane costumes designed to disguise the human form when they handle or are around cranes."

The cranes were raised to follow an ultralight aircraft with a pilot wearing a crane costume. Prior to hatching, staff played recordings of ultralight aircraft engine sounds for the eggs. When they first arrived at Necedah, the young cranes were led around a track by the ultralight driving on the ground. When the young whooping cranes fledged to their flying feathers, they were taken on training flights led by the ultralight in the hopes that the aircraft could lead them on a migration to a national wildlife refuge on the Gulf Coast of Florida.

Whooping crane migration is a behavior that must be learned. In the wild, cranes learn from their parents. Conservationists hoped that cranes who learned a migration route from an ultralight aircraft in the fall would return north on their own when spring came. The ultralight-led migration from Wisconsin to Florida required a great deal of coordination and support. Landowners along the route acted as "stopover hosts," giving the cranes, and the team of humans following them, a safe and private overnight resting place on their way south. The idea had been demonstrated a year before with sandhill cranes, which have an abundant population in the hundreds of thousands in North America.

In the fall of the inaugural year of the Whooping Crane Project, the first class of cranes was ready to be led south. They were seven in number. The 1,200-mile southward migration began on October 17, 2001. They all arrived safely forty-eight days later, arriving on December 3. That winter, two of the birds were taken out by wild bobcats.

Then, on April 9, 2002, the five remaining whooping cranes that had been led south by the ultralight and survived the winter in Florida took off and headed north on their own. They had transmitters on their legs to be tracked by the project team.

Two days of rain soon grounded the migrating cranes in Georgia. They then, on their own, resumed their migration. The birds would not fly over a body of water if they could not see the other side, so when they hit the southern tip of Lake

Michigan, they had to decide to fly eastward toward the state of Michigan or westward toward Wisconsin. They flew westward. The human team that was following them got stuck in traffic on the Dan Ryan Expressway on the south side of Chicago and lost track of the cranes. A dentist in Chicago, who knew about this extraordinary science fair project to reestablish a whooping crane population east of the Mississippi River, saw the cranes and reported them to the right people. The cranes had put down for the night north of Chicago in a quarry that had filled with water from a recent rain. The next day, they continued their flight north. On April 19, eleven days after leaving Florida, they arrived at the wildlife refuge in Wisconsin where they had been raised.

I became familiar with the program to reestablish a migrating whooping crane population when the head of Watchable Wildlife, a nonprofit organization headquartered in Minnesota, and I began researching the idea of an IMAX film on the crane project. We spent time with a great deal of staff, hid in blinds to watch cranes go through flight training behind ultralights at the Necedah Refuge, and brought IMAX film directors to Wisconsin to help study the feasibility of the idea.

Not all documentary film ideas, even after thorough research and scouting, come to fruition. In the case of the whooping cranes, there were too many essential protocols surrounding the birds' rearing, training, and migrating to add to the mix a film crew documenting the effort in the world's largest film format. At that time, IMAX cameras were big and noisy and had a magazine limit of three minutes of film. The Whooping Crane Migration Project was early in its operation and not ready to integrate an IMAX film team, adding unknown factors to an already complicated and critical conservation effort. We had to respect the magnitude of the reintroduction initiative and abandon the film idea. We would have been an interference.

The Whooping Crane Reintroduction Project changed course after fifteen years, ending the ultralight-led migrations. While it was successful in establishing a new migrating group of cranes, for reasons not understood, the cranes had little success breeding and raising young in the wild. Power line collisions and predators also hindered the growth of the migrating population. And while at the beginning of 2007 the reintroduced migratory population was more than eighty, seventeen of eighteen young birds that had just completed their ultralight-led migration to Florida were killed by severe storms in the early morning hours of February 2.

Like many others, I hope the cranes on their own can grow a migrating group without the costume-rearing, human intervention approach. By 2020, an estimated one hundred whooping cranes were summering in Wisconsin and nearby states and making an annual migration on their own. The long-term results of this extraordinary project are still to be determined.

AN HOUR DRIVE SOUTHWEST of the Necedah National Wildlife Refuge and thirty miles east of LaCrosse, Wisconsin, another Mississippi River town amid the Driftless Area, is a ten-mile roadway that connects Cashton and Ontario, Wisconsin. More than two thousand Amish live around this stretch of roadway. On one drive my spouse and I stopped at a roadside bakery along the route. On a hot summer day, Amish women worked inside in their long sleeves and long dresses. We said we were shopping for quilts. They suggested we go to Grandma Shrock's house, and they pulled out a pencil and drew a map on a piece of paper.

The Shrocks' farmstead was off the state roadway, and there were no signs advertising quilts for sale. They did have a building at the front of the property that served as the quilt showroom.

CONSERVATION COUNTRY

The sign on the door read, "Ring bell." I looked for the doorbell where an English person like myself would expect it to be, but no doorbell. I looked down and around the frame of the door without seeing a button. Then I looked up. There, I saw the bell—much like a church bell with a pull cord to ring it. When I did, two young, barefoot Amish boys ran up to us. They led us into the building, which had three beds with dozens of quilts piled neatly on them. They politely turned the quilts back one at a time so that we could examine each. They told us Grandma Shrock was away at a family funeral, so we would have to come back another day.

Upon our return trip, we stopped at the farmstead and rang the bell. The same two boys appeared. They spoke English and smiled and giggled. Then Grandma Shrock showed up. She spoke tersely to the boys in the Amish German dialect, and they stiffened up and let her do the talking from that point on. As with any transaction with the Amish, we had the option to pay cash or write a check. We came home with two beautiful quilts.

A few years later, we decided we wanted another quilt and stopped again at Grandma Shrock's. There was no bell to ring. I looked in the window and the showroom was empty. We saw a group of Amish men working outside at a barn next door and headed over to their farmstead. The men said that Grandma Shrock had passed away, but her daughter had taken over the quilting operation. We got another pencil-drawn map and made off to the daughter's farmstead.

Grandma Shrock's adult daughter came out and met us at her showroom at the front of the property, again with three beds and piles of quilts. A heavy storm was coming in and it was getting quite dark. The woman shouted to her daughter to bring a lantern. It was the first time I have ever shopped by kerosene lamp.

While my wife was looking at quilts, I thought I could get

creative about connecting and take advantage of the opportunity to learn more about the Amish by engaging in a conversation with Grandma Shrock's granddaughter. I asked her if she went to school. Before she could say anything, her mother quickly and tersely spoke. "No, she's thirteen. She's done now." I didn't attempt to continue the conversation. I had to be mindful, suspend my judgement, not overreact, and most importantly, be respectful of the people I just met. We bought another beautiful quilt, wished the mother and daughter well, and went on our way content to know the Shrocks were conserving their lifestyle in conservation country.

Chapter 19

THE PLEASANTEST SENSATION IN THE WORLD

MINNESOTA

FREYA STARK WAS BORN in Paris in 1893 and lived to be one hundred. She left behind twenty-four books of her travels that the *New York Times* referenced as "lucid, spontaneous and elegant." A godson wrote that she saw travel "as the pursuit of truth." She made trips through the Middle East to places no westerner had ever been, including one trip in Syria with another woman, and an ethnic Druze guide, traveling at night on donkeys. Dame Freya Madeline Stark once wrote, "To awaken in a strange town is one of the pleasantest sensations in the world."

In February 2020, my bride and I awoke in a palapa on a cliffside overlooking the Pacific Ocean near the town of Sayulita in Mexico's state of Nayarit. You can board any of scores of flights to destinations in Mexico from Minneapolis in February. We flew to Puerto Vallarta. I remember before catching our flight back to Minnesota, taking a seat on the concourse and watching the sea of humanity that, like us, had come to this part of the world for a winter getaway.

People streamed by in tropical shirts, shorts or loose pants, sandals or soft shoes, and sunburns. We were only a few weeks away from Major League Baseball's spring training and, for us, another flight out of Minneapolis to another warm weather destination—Florida. We sat in the Puerto Vallarta airport and began discussing a winter getaway for the following year. I never imagined it would be 487 days before I would again get on an airplane. No spring training. No palapas. No leaving the United States. Not even a drive across the border to Canada, let alone a flight to Europe, Asia, or Africa. SARS-CoV-2, the virus that caused COVID-19, had become a stowaway on airplanes.

A viable hope for the world would be vaccines to combat the virus. On December 19, 2020, nine months after the World Health Organization declared a pandemic, the prime minister of Israel went on live TV and became the first person in that country to receive a shot of the Pfizer vaccine. The next day in Israel, people over the age of sixty, those at high risk, and those who worked in healthcare received a text with a phone number to call to make an appointment for their own vaccinations. If you were a senior, but your spouse was not, he or she was invited to come with you and get a shot. Within three weeks, 20 percent of the country's population had the first of the vaccine's two-dose regimen. Come early February 2021, more than 90 percent of Israelis over the age of sixty had received at least one dose of the vaccine. This resulted in a 40 percent drop in confirmed COVID cases compared to one month before.

In early January 2021, the US federal government urged US states to offer the COVID vaccine to anyone age sixty-five and older. Two days later, the State of Minnesota announced they would move forward accordingly after vaccinating residents and workers in long-term care facilities. The state invited those eligible to go to a website the following week to sign up for an appointment at one of nine pilot vaccination sites. The Minnesota COVID vaccine race began. A colleague in Saint Paul and I discussed how we were going to be ready at noon that day—the moment registration opened.

PRIMARY BIO, A STATE contractor, built and operated Minnesota's COVID vaccination registration website. At the appointed hour on opening day, I logged on to sign up. I quickly reached a screen labeled "Waiting Room." My colleague, who was working on two computers and an iPad, had the same experience. While we waited, I followed updates on the status of the enrollment program on Twitter on my phone.

At the time, there were more than eight hundred thousand seniors living outside of long-term care facilities in Minnesota. To accommodate the numbers as efficiently as possible, the pilot sites would operate from Thursday through Sunday, with six thousand appointments available the first week. When registration opened, the website received more than two thousand hits per second. The site crashed in its first hour of operation.

Twitter reports advised that those in the waiting room should stay there. My colleague and I did that—for four hours. After four hours, we clicked the back button to step back a page and found ourselves on the page that allowed us to make appointments. By then, eight of the nine pilot sites were full. I made an appointment at the only site that still had availability.

My appointment for my first vaccine shot was on Friday, January 22, 2021, at 4:00 p.m. at the Franklin Middle School in Thief River Falls, Minnesota. Thief River Falls is 265 miles west of the North Shore of Lake Superior, where I was staying during the pandemic. Driving across northern Minnesota in January had never been on my travel bucket list. But after staying close to home for almost a year, the appointment provided a dual opportunity—first to get a COVID vaccine, and second to get out and see a part of the world I'd never experienced before. As Scottish novelist, poet, and travel writer Robert Louis Stevenson, author of *Treasure Island*, once wrote, "I travel not to go anywhere, but to go. The great affair is to move."

My drive to Thief River Falls in the depths of January took five hours. I arrived safely and checked into the AmericInn. It was the first night I had spent in a hotel since our holiday on the Pacific Ocean in Mexico eleven months before. The desk clerk told me the pool was open. I never planned on sitting in a hot tub with other guests during a pandemic, so I hadn't packed a bathing suit. I had, however, packed my Clorox disinfecting wipes. I used them to sanitize the TV remote, anticipating that I'd spend the evening ahead in self-quarantine following my vaccine jab.

I showed up, masked, for my 4:00 p.m. appointment. Upon my check-in, the site staff gave me a blue surgical mask, instructing me to wear it in addition to my own mask. Now double masked, I snaked my way through the middle school gymnasium to a registration desk operated by a uniformed member of the Minnesota National Guard. He confirmed my appointment on his laptop, as well as the place and time of my second appointment: Saturday, February 13. He then directed me to one of eight lines, where I stood and waited to receive the vaccine.

The nurse who gave me my shot was friendly. She was from Grand Forks, North Dakota, and had been traveling for weeks to administer these shots. She said she was happy to be doing so. The process was quick and efficient, and I received proof of vaccination—my coveted COVID-19 Vaccination Record Card with a sticker listing the lot number and dosage of the Pfizer vaccine I received. I retreated to the AmericInn for the night, planning to drive back to the North Shore of Lake Superior the next day, and got caught up on a TV news broadcast from Grand Forks.

After an uneventful night, I woke up early. The hotel didn't serve its usual hot breakfast offerings due to the pandemic, nor did it allow guests to sit in the dining area. It did offer limited food selections to take away. I took a bagel, a banana, yogurt, and a hard-boiled egg and filled my Yeti travel mug from the coffee urn. I checked out of the hotel and headed out to my car in the subzero temperatures. Sitting in the dark of a northern Minnesota winter morning in my very cold car as I waited for it to warm up, I muttered the words of Dame Freya Stark, "To awaken in a strange town is one of the pleasantest sensations in the world."

As I began my drive across the frozen darkness of northwest Minnesota, I turned on a podcast. Down the road a way, I took my first drink of hot coffee—it was the worst coffee I ever tasted. It might have been made the day before and been left sitting in the hotel urn overnight.

At first light, almost an hour into my drive, I went through the town of Fosston, Minnesota. In the frigid early morning, it looked like a ghost town. As I looked to my right at the marquee of the single-screen movie theater on the main street (*Croods 2* was playing), I caught a glimpse of the only illuminated sign within view on the other side of the road: Caribou Coffee Drive-Thru.

Caribou began in the 1990s in Minnesota and had been my go-to coffee place for years. I had the Caribou app on my phone and money in my account. I circled my car around a few blocks to make sure I wouldn't miss where the drive-through entrance was. On that dark, cold, COVID morning, Fosston looked like a movie set waiting for its crew to show up. I stopped the car and went to my Caribou app. It asked for a password, probably because I hadn't used it in the ten months of the pandemic. I couldn't remember what it was, but I still had currency in my wallet that had gone unspent for months.

I ordered a "skinny, hot latte as big as you can make it." I decided to celebrate my adventure and added an apple fritter to my order. My usual diet, void of baked goods, had been thrown out the window in the early months of the pandemic. My total came to less than $7.

I pulled up to the pick-up window, gave the barista a Jackson—a $20 bill—and told her to keep the change. I couldn't remember the last time I had used US paper currency for a transaction. I drove out of Fosston with what I still believe is the best cup of coffee I have ever tasted.

I HAD SUSPECTED THAT Israel's smooth and efficient administration of vaccines would not be replicated in the US. My experience scrambling for a first shot, with its confusing messaging and technical glitches, gave credence to that suspicion. What happened next confirmed it.

When I had registered for a first dose, I was able to make an appointment for a second dose three weeks later at the pilot site closest to home. My next journey would take me to Buhl High School in Mountain Iron, Minnesota, eighty-five miles from our North Shore cabin.

During the second week of vaccine availability the state announced they were changing the program. All the more than 790,000 seniors who had not yet been vaccinated could register online for a vaccine lottery that began at 5 a.m. on Tuesday, January 26. More than 225,000 seniors signed up.

The following Saturday, more than a week after I had received my first shot at the Thief River Falls pilot site, I got a text message that read, "MDH COVID-19 Vaccine Pilot Program: You were able to make a vaccine appointment even though you were not randomly selected. As a result, we regret to inform you that your appointment is unauthorized and no longer valid.

IMPORTANT: Please do not visit any vaccine pilot location. Walk-ins are not accepted and you do not have an appointment at this time."

That morning, the Twin Cities media reported that they were hearing from others who had been notified by the Department of Health that their second-dose appointments had been canceled. In one case someone received seventeen copies of the same email.

Shortly after noon that day, I received another text: "This morning you received a message from us indicating your appointment was unauthorized and invalid. That was an ERROR and we sincerely apologize for any confusion." The Minnesota Department of Health blamed Primary Bio for the erroneous texts and emails. The contractor's mistake had resulted in mass confusion and frustration—and not much resolution.

A few days later, the state announced that seniors would be able to get their vaccine shots from local health providers or at large-scale vaccination sites. The Twin Cities' ABC affiliate reported, "The Minnesota Department of Health now has its *third* vaccination plan in three weeks." Its first large-scale vaccination sites would open in Minneapolis and Duluth. Minnesota Public Radio reported that these sites would "replace nine pilot clinics the state set up last month to administer vaccines to people age sixty-five and older who preregistered with the state's lottery system. For those who received their first doses at one of the pilot sites, they will be contacted to schedule an appointment for their second shot." The confusion continued. I reminded myself of a traveler's life lesson: you cannot best understand the world until you surrender to its apparent chaotic reality. Then you get to better know the parts that you have to play with.

In the early days of February, I checked my email and text messages regularly, expecting to receive instructions for my approaching second dose. When I hadn't been contacted by

Thursday, February 11, I called Buhl High School in Mountain Iron, the site for my scheduled second dose appointment two days later. I reached someone in the office and asked if the school was still a site for vaccine shots, as I had heard they might not be anymore. The woman who answered my call said, "Well, the National Guard is here today, and they better not be here for anything other than those COVID shots." The next evening, the evening before my scheduled second shot, I received an email *and* a text that confirmed my appointment at Buhl for the following afternoon.

On Saturday, February 13, 2021, I drove two hours from Knife River to Mountain Iron, which calls itself the "Taconite Capital of the World." There is a statue of Leonidas Merritt in front of the library, the person credited with the discovery of iron ore here in 1890. I had time before my appointment to stop at the "Historic Overlook," a park where you view the open pit mine. No one had plowed the walkways, so I made my way through the deep snow up to the fence for the view. The Leonidas Merritt Days festival is held each August in the park.

Mountain Iron is the home to the first open pit mine on the Mesabi Iron Ore Range in Minnesota. In 1988, it was also the site of the first class-action sexual harassment lawsuit ever filed in the United States, brought by a group of women against one of the mining companies. The history was documented in the 2002 published book *Class Action*. Charlize Theron's 2005 movie *North Country*, a fictionalized story of the lawsuit, features stunning filming of the mines of the Range.

Fifteen minutes after I arrived in Mountain Iron, after many websites visited, texts and emails received, questions asked, hours spent, and miles logged, I was fully vaccinated against COVID. A mixture of dogged persistence and tolerating, even embracing, the inevitable uncertainties of life in the United

States during a pandemic had culminated in a moment that was at once anticlimactic and enormously meaningful.

A nurse who had traveled from a hospital in Duluth gave me my jab, then added the dosage information to my COVID-19 Vaccination Record Card. She handed it to me and said, "Here is your golden ticket."

I looked at her and said, "Few are the giants of the soul who feel that the human race is their family circle," words written by Freya Stark.

ACKNOWLEDGMENTS

THANK YOU TO THE writers, editors, designers, and management and marketing professionals that made this book possible. Your talents and dedication to the craft have been a privilege to work with.

My sincere thanks to Victoria Petelin, Kerry Stapley, Sarah Imholte, Steven Woodward, Hanna Kjeldbjerg, Crown Shepherd, Karen Callan, and Vivian Steckline.

I am blessed to have thirteen nieces and nephews who have always welcomed going on an adventure and been the most joyful of travel companions. And to have a beautiful bride who has given us the best mantra for the inevitable challenging and frustrating moments of travel—we pause, take a deep breath, and say, "As long as we get there safe."